Awaking Beauty

A musical

Book and lyrics by Alan Ayckbourn
Music by Denis King

Samuel French — London
www.samuelfrench-london.co.uk

ISBN 978 0 573 18002 6

AWAKING BEAUTY

First produced at The Stephen Joseph Theatre, Scarborough on 16th December 2008 with the following cast of characters:

Carabosse	Anna Francolini
The Prince	Duncan Patrick
Princess Aurora	Alice Fearn
The Pigcutter	Ben Fox
First Narrator	Verity Quade
Second Narrator	Annalene Beechey
Third Narrator	Helen French
Fourth Narrator	Matthew White
Fifth Narrator	Ian McLarnon
Sixth Narrator	Jon-Paul Hevey

Directed by Alan Ayckbourn
Designed by Michael Holt

COPYRIGHT INFORMATION

(See also page ii)

Licences for amateur performances are issued subject to the understanding that it shall be made clear in all advertising matter that the audience will witness an amateur performance; that the names of the authors of the plays shall be included on all programmes; and that the integrity of the authors' work will be preserved.

The Royalty Fee is subject to contract and subject to variation at the sole discretion of Samuel French Ltd.

In Theatres or Halls seating Four Hundred or more the fee will be subject to negotiation.

In Territories Overseas the fee quoted above may not apply. A fee will be quoted on application to our local authorized agent, or if there is no such agent, on application to Samuel French Ltd, London.

VIDEO-RECORDING OF AMATEUR PRODUCTIONS

Please note that the copyright laws governing video-recording are extremely complex and that it should not be assumed that any play may be video-recorded for whatever purpose without first obtaining the permission of the appropriate agents. The fact that a play is published by Samuel French Ltd does not indicate that video rights are available or that Samuel French Ltd controls such rights.

CHARACTERS

Carabosse
The Prince
Princess Aurora
The Pigcutter
First Narrator (female) also playing **Maurice De Vine, Woman 1, Woman 4**
Second Narrator (female) also playing **Woman 2, Woman 5, Second Beautician, Miss Chasum**
Third Narrator (female) also playing **Woman 3, Woman 6, Beauty Salon Assistant, Third Hairdresser, Midwife, Supermarket Girl**
Fourth Narrator (male) also playing **The Grand Sorceress, First Prince, Man 1, Man 4, Beauty Salon Manager, First Hairdresser, Baby Conrad**
Fifth Narrator (male) also playing **Second Prince, Man 2, Man 5, Estate Agent, First Beautician, Baby Boris**
Sixth Narrator (male) also playing **Third Prince, Man 3, Man 6, Second Hairdresser, Geoff, Baby Arthur**

SYNOPSIS OF SCENES

PROLOGUE A bare stage

ACT I Scene 1 Carabosse's cave
Scene 2 The Grand Hall of Sorcerers
Scene 3 The grounds of Princess Aurora's Castle
Scene 4 Carabosse's cave
Scene 5 A street somewhere in the Big City
Scene 6 An Estate Agent's office
Scene 7 A reception of a hairdressing salon and beauty clinic

ENTR'ACTE A bare stage

ACT II Scene 1 A bare stage
Scene 2 The hospital waiting-room
Scene 3 The City streets
Scene 4 The bedroom at 29 Brown Brick Road
Scene 5 The City streets
Scene 6 Living-area of a dingy self-catering hotel room
Scene 7 The sitting-room at 29 Brown Brick Road

EPILOGUE The interior of the cave

Time—more recently than you think

MUSICAL NUMBERS

ACT I

No. 1 This Has To Be Love (**Prince**, **Aurora**, **Carabosse**)
No. 2 Aurora's Vow (**Aurora**)
No. 3 Do Your Worst (**Carabosse**, **Prince**)
No. 4 Aurora's Vow (reprise) (**Aurora**)
No. 5 Particular (**Pigcutter**)
No. 6 Love Comes Later (**Sorceress**)
No. 7 Busy in the City (**Narrators**)
No. 8 Welcome (**De Vine** and **Narrators**)

ACT II

No. 9 This Has To Be Love (version 5) (**Prince**, **Aurora**)
No. 10 Particular (reprise) (**Pigcutter**)
No. 11 Awaking Beauty (**De Vine** and **Narrators**)
No. 12 The Laughing Song (**Miss Chasum** and **Carabosse**)
No. 13 Multiple Birth Refrain (**Prince**, **Aurora**, **Narrators**)
No. 14 Busy in the City Reprise (**Narrators**)
No. 15 Only Then (**Carabosse** and **Pigcutter**)
No. 16 Aurora's Lullaby (**Aurora** and **Narrators**)
No. 17 The World to Me (**Aurora**)
No. 18 I'll Settle for You (**Carabosse** and **Pigcutter**)

The vocal score is available on hire from Samuel French Ltd

Other plays by Alan Ayckbourn published by Samuel French Ltd

Absent Friends
Absurd Person Singular
Bedroom Farce
Body Language
Callisto 5
The Champion of Paribanou
A Chorus of Disapproval
Comic Potential
Communicating Doors
Confusions
A Cut in the Rates
Damsels in Distress (trilogy: FlatSpin, GamePlan, RolePlay)
Dreams from a Summer House (music by John Pattison)
Drowning on Dry Land
Ernie's Incredible Illucinations
Family Circles
Garden
Gizmo
Henceforward ...
House
House & Garden
How the Other Half Loves
Improbable Fiction (music by Denis King)
Intimate Exchanges (Volume I)
Intimate Exchanges (Volume II)
Invisible Friends
It Could Be Any One of Us
Joking Apart
Just Between Ourselves
Living Together
Man of the Moment
Mixed Doubles
Mr A's Amazing Maze Plays
Mr Whatnot
My Very Own Story
The Norman Conquests
Orvin — Champion of Champions (music by Denis King)
Relatively Speaking
The Revengers' Comedies
Round and Round the Garden
Season's Greetings
Sisterly Feelings
A Small Family Business
Snake in the Grass
Suburban Strains (music by Paul Todd)
Table Manners
Taking Steps
Ten Times Table
Things We Do For Love
This Is Where We Came In
Time and Time Again
Time of My Life
Tons of Money (revised version)
Way Upstream
Whenever (music by Denis King)
Wildest Dreams
Wolf at the Door (adapted from Henri Becque's *Les Corbeaux*)
Woman in Mind
A Word from Our Sponsor (music by John Pattison)

PROLOGUE

The Lights come up on an empty stage

A brief overture. At the conclusion, the Lights fade to a black-out

Carabosse and the six Narrators enter in the darkness. The Narrators remain on stage throughout the play

Unaccompanied, the voices of the six Narrators start up, gradually joining together wordlessly, until they reach a dramatic opening chord. Then a light comes up on the Narrators

Narrators And so the story goes …

The other Narrators continue softly, wordlessly under the following

First Narrator And whether you first heard it five years ago or fifty years ago, you will certainly remember it. How the Princess Aurora, having pricked her finger on the spindle, at once fell asleep along with the whole royal palace for a hundred years. And how, as she slept, her wicked godmother Carabosse, who had cast the spell, watched and gloated.

A light comes up briefly on Carabosse

Carabosse Ha-ha-ha-ha-ha-ha!

The light goes down on her again

The Narrators continue under the following

First Narrator As years passed, inside the palace the dust settled deeper and the cobwebs denser, for only the spiders had escaped the witch's spell. Outside in the grounds the grass grew high, the trees tall and the brambles grew everywhere until it was impossible for any living soul to approach the palace without being scratched and torn to pieces by the thorns. Though many brave noblemen tried —

The Fourth Narrator steps forward

Fourth Narrator (*as a prince, reacting to the brambles*) Ah-ah-ah-ah-ow! (*He retreats*)

The Fifth Narrator steps forward

Fifth Narrator (*likewise*) Ah-ah-ah-ah-ow! (*He retreats, also defeated*)

First Narrator And the witch, Carabosse, loved watching all these splendid noblemen being torn and scratched to pieces. And she laughed and laughed ...

A light comes up again briefly on Carabosse

Carabosse Ha-ha-ha-ha-ha-ha!

The light goes down on her again

The Narrators continue under the following

First Narrator And it seemed that nowhere in the kingdom did there live a prince or a knight, not a single nobleman, however brave, who could possibly rescue the sleeping princess. Until one day from a far distant land —

The Prince enters

The Narrators do a short vocal fanfare

A magnificent, fearless prince arrived.

Prince (*fearlessly*) Ha! Ha! (*He stands impressively, surveying the palace and the task ahead*)

The Narrators continue under the following

First Narrator This was a prince not to be frightened by a few thorns and brambles!

Prince (*contemptuously*) Ba!

First Narrator If there was a beautiful princess in need of rescue, here stood the man to rescue her! Without a moment's hesitation, the Prince set off through the dense undergrowth —

Prince Ho! Ho! (*He strides forward*)

The Narrators become the undergrowth. They move forward with a menacing, threatening brambly sound to block the Prince's path. They sway and lash out at him

Narrators Aaaahhh! Aaaahhh! Aaaahhh!
Prince (*reacting to this*) Ow! Ow! Ouch! Ow!
First Narrator — and the witch watched wickedly —–

A light comes up again briefly on Carabosse

Carabosse Ha-ha-ha-ha-ha-ha!

The light goes down on her again. The Prince battles on

First Narrator For she knew that no mortal man, however brave, could ever pass through her barrier of thorns ...
All Aaaahhh! Aaaahhh! Aaaahhh!
Prince Oh, bugger!
First Narrator But this prince from a far off land was no ordinary prince. He was the bravest, most courageous of princes who wasn't going to let a few mere brambles get the better of him. What's more — he had a trusty sword!

The Prince draws his sword

Prince Ha! ha!
Narrators (*drawing back at the sight of his sword*) Aaaaahhh!
First Narrator Even the wicked witch was impressed ...

A light comes up again briefly on Carabosse

Carabosse (*seeing the sword*) Ooooh!

The light goes out on her again

First Narrator And suddenly the Prince began to win the battle against the vicious brambles …
Prince (*swishing his sword*) Take that! And that! And that!
Narrators (*reacting and recoiling under his onslaught, variously*) Ow! Ow! Ouch! Ow! Oh, bugger!
First Narrator ... until all was cleared and he finally reached the door of the castle itself.
Prince (*triumphantly*) Ha! ha!

A silence. The Narrators have retreated into the shadows. The Prince stands alone in an isolated light

First Narrator (*whispering*) The Prince found himself standing in front of a huge door. Cautiously, he pushed it open ...

The Prince mimes opening the door. The Narrators supply the sound as he does so, as they will do throughout, half musically, half onomatopoeically

Narrators Eeeeee-e-e-e-e-e-e-e-eeek!
First Narrator And he entered the silent castle. As he did so, the door behind him swung to again ...
Narrators Eeeeee-e-e-e-e-e-e-e-eeek!
First Narrator ... and slammed shut!
Narrators Du-n-n-n-k-k!
First Narrator Which startled the prince.
Prince (*jumping*) Oh!
First Narrator For a while the Prince could see and hear nothing but as he moved forward, his eyes grew used to the darkness ...

As the Prince reaches the other individual Narrators, each one is briefly lit. All stand in frozen positions, as if caught in mid-action

Everyone in the palace, masters, manservants, mistresses and maids ... had been frozen in time, as they had been for a hundred years ... As the Prince moved further into the palace and his ears became accustomed to the silence, beyond the darkness, he could hear hundreds of tiny noises —
Narrators (*a soft rustling*) Scutter-scutter-scutter-scutter-scutter —
First Narrator — as a thousand spiders busily worked away, weaving a million webs ...
Narrators Scutter-scutter-scutter-scutter-scutter —
Prince (*repulsed*) Uuuugghh!
First Narrator And the Prince hurried in his search to find the sleeping Princess ...

The Prince continues to move round, passing the various Narrators in frozen poses

But although he searched everywhere, passing cooks and valets, footmen and gardeners, butlers and chambermaids ... The Prince was unable to find Princess Aurora anywhere. He was almost ready to give up when, at the end of a passageway, he came to a door he'd missed the first time ...

The Prince mimes opening a door

Narrators (*a creak*) Eeeeee-e-e-e-e-e-e-e-eeek!

A bed rises up with Princess Aurora asleep on it

The Narrators greet its appearance musically. They continue softly under the next

First Narrator And so he found her. The Prince moved closer to her bed in wonder, scarcely able to believe his eyes. She was truly the most beautiful Princess he had ever seen in his life. And then and there, before he'd had time to draw another breath, the Prince fell completely and utterly in love.

No. 1 This Has To Be Love

Prince (*singing, softly at first*) This has be love!
Up here, my head feels both delighted and dizzy
Down there, things are getting excited and busy
She's not yet awoken, we haven't yet spoken
Yet I know, yes I know,
That this really and truly,
My passion's unruly,
This certainly has to be love!

A light again briefly on Carabosse

Carabosse (*speaking disgustedly*) Yuurrrkkk!

Prince (*singing*) This has to be love!
My vision is blurred and my poor head is pounding,
Her lips are divine and her breasts quite astounding,
My heart feels it's broken, could this be a token?
Yes, I know, it is so
That this certainly, clearly,
No, not even nearly,
It's got to be, has to be love!

A light again briefly on Carabosse

Carabosse (*speaking disgustedly*) Yuurrrkkk!

Prince (*singing*) I've had this recurring dream
The way romance would feel;
Now, suddenly it would seem,
This whole thing is for real —
It has to be love!

Though I have no idea of her name I concede it,
If the rest of her body's the same, then I need it!
I'll gently awake her, and woo her and make her,
Till I swear that by heaven above,
Very soon she'll agree with me
It has to be love.

First Narrator And the witch, who had enough of this, was about to cast a really horrible spell on them to turn them both into stag beetles so she could stamp on them and have done with it — but before she could say so much as an abracadabra ...

The Prince steps forward and kisses Aurora gently on the lips. The Narrators' underscore swells to a sweet crescendo. The Prince steps back as Aurora stirs and wakes up. She sleepily opens her eyes and sees the Prince

Aurora (*singing*) This has to be love!
I awake from a dream that was mildly exotic,
To a kiss, I confess, I found wildly erotic,
My whole body's burning my insides are churning,
Yes, of this I was warned,
Long ago by my nanny
It's simply uncanny,
This certainly has to be love!

A light again briefly on Carabosse

Carabosse (*speaking*) I'm putting a stop to this ...

As the underscore builds again, all but drowning out the disgusted Carabosse, the Prince starts to take off his clothes; Aurora lies back imploringly, her arms stretched out to him

Both This has to be love!
It's love at first sight, with our two hearts combining,
Our bodies will follow, our parts intertwining,

Prince This has to be it!
Aurora You're sure it will fit?
Both That this really and truly,
Our passion's unruly,
This certainly has to be love!

Until the Prince is stripped down to his medieval briefs. Aurora stares at him entranced. The music stops abruptly. Carabosse also stares at the Prince, transfixed

First Narrator And then just as the couple were about to love happily ever after, the most extraordinary thing happened.
Carabosse (*softly*) Oh, dear God! (*She sings*)

This has to be —
Prince, Aurora — love!
Carabosse This has to be —
Prince, Aurora — love at first sight, with our two hearts combining,
Our bodies will follow, our parts intertwining,

The Prince and Aurora continue singing to each other regardless, he approaching the bed preparing to lie with her

Prince This really is it!
Aurora I'm sure it will fit.
Both That this really and truly,
Our passion's unruly,
This certainly has to be — !

As they prepare to engage, Carabosse stops the proceedings

Carabosse (*speaking vehemently*) No! No! No! No! NO!

The music stops

First Narrator And the infuriated Carabosse resolved, if she wasn't to have the Prince herself, to turn them both into bluebottles to be eaten by the hungry spiders. But before she could do this —
Aurora (*wriggling out from under the Prince*) Darling ... sorry I — (*Climbing off the bed*) Won't be the briefest tick.
Prince (*perturbed*) Where are you going?

Aurora To the ... Sorry. It has been a hundred years, I'm simply bursting ...
Prince Oh, right. Of course ...
Aurora Don't go away ...

Aurora scampers off

The Prince lies with his eyes closed

First Narrator At this, Carabosse seized her opportunity —
Carabosse Ha-ha-ha-ha-ha-ha!

The light fades on Carabosse

Carabosse exits

All (*a magic sound*) Waaaaahhhhh!

Immediately, Aurora, now as Carabosse, returns

Aurora (*Carabosse's laugh*) Ha-ha-ha-ha-ha-ha!

The Prince opens his eyes, startled

Prince What?
Aurora Back again.
Prince So soon.
Aurora I don't hang about.

From the bathroom there is the sound of banging on the door and faint calls from Aurora

Prince What's that?
Aurora What?
Prince That noise? What is it?
Aurora Just the plumbing. (*Snuggling up to him*) Hallo, beautiful. Where were we, then?

The Narrators resume the underscore

Oh yes ... (*She sings*)

This has to be love!

The Prince, somewhat bewildered, joins with her

Prince This has to be —
Both Love at first sight, with our two hearts combining,
Our bodies are close now, our parts intertwining,
Prince It certainly fits
Aurora Get a load of these tits ...
Both That this really and truly,
Our passion's unruly,
This certainly has to be love!

The couple on the bed start to make love, Aurora somewhat more vigorously and enthusiastically than the Prince expected. As the whole thing looks as it might get out of hand, the Narrators gather hastily around the bed shielding it from view

The Prince and Aurora disappear as the bed descends again during the rest of the song

Narrators That this really and truly,
Their passion's unruly,
This certainly has to be love!

The song ends

The Narrators disperse and the Second Narrator takes up the tale

Second Narrator After a magical night filled with vigorous love, the blissful couple fell into a deep sleep and they both dreamt of living happily ever after.

The Narrators commence a dawn underscore, complete with birds etc. the full works, under the following

And as dawn broke, the sun peeped through the windows and, seeing the slumbering lovers, smiled to himself and discreetly drew a soft white cloud over his face for fear he would disturb them. Outside in the garden, the birds gradually returned to find that where there had been prickly brambles and sharp thorns, there now grew huge lawns and beautiful flowers and tall trees.

The bed rises. Only the sleeping Prince is visible, Carabosse, as Aurora, is invisible under the bedclothes

As the underscore continues, the Prince wakes up. He looks around him, alarmed there is no sign of Aurora. He smiles as he becomes aware of her in the bed beside him. He touches her sleeping shape through the blanket affectionately, not wishing to disturb her, yet. He sings softly to himself at first but, as his heart takes flight, eventually so does his song. The Narrators gently add an accompaniment

Prince (*growing gradually louder*) This has to be love!
Up here, my head feels both delighted and dizzy
Down there, things are getting excited and busy
She's not yet awoken, we haven't yet spoken
Yet I know, yes I know,
That this really and truly,
My passion's unruly,
This certainly has to be —

Carabosse (*speaking, muffled, from under the covers*) Oy! Keep the noise down, lover boy.

The music stops

Prince I'm sorry. What did you say, my love?
Carabosse (*in very much her own voice*) I'm trying to get some kip down here.
Prince What? Aurora, my beloved? (*Becoming a trifle alarmed*) Aurora?
Second Narrator When the Prince drew back the bedclothes imagine his dismay when he saw —

The Prince draws back the bedclothes to reveal Carabosse. He stares in horror

Narrators (*dramatic chord of revelation*) Daaaaa!
Carabosse (*smiling, sleepily*) 'Morning.
Prince AAAAaaaaahhhh! (*He leaps out of bed, still in his underwear*) Get away! Get away from me, you vile creature!
Carabosse Eh?
Prince You filthy, disgusting hag, what are you doing in that bed?
Carabosse You've changed your tune from last night, haven't you?
Prince Last night?
Carabosse (*singing*) "This has to be love!" ... (*Speaking*) Very different story in the morning, isn't it?
Prince That wasn't you, you foul, repellent monster! Look at you, just take a look at yourself!

Carabosse I can promise you, darling, I'm exactly the same as I was — (*Catching sight of her hand and realizing*) Oh! I've changed back. It's worn off in the night.
Prince Hideous creature!
Carabosse But I'm still the same, I just look different. It's still me, lover. (*Extending her arms to him*) Come here, I'll prove it to you.
Prince Keep away from me, vile witch. I would sooner stroke a toad!
Carabosse (*getting out of bed, excitedly*) How can you say that? Look it's me! Me! It was a night we vowed never to forget? We both said it, lying there in the darkness. Don't you remember?
Prince Where is my beloved? What have you done with her?
Carabosse She's here! She's over here, you fool!
Prince You? I could never love you. Never in a million years, you repulse me, you repel me, you distorted, hideous — thing! (*Calling*) Aurora! Aurora! My darling Aurora!

He starts to put on his clothes. Carabosse watches him rather stunned

Second Narrator And the witch, although she was well over three hundred years old, still knew very little about men and particularly men the morning after. But she was beginning to learn.
Carabosse Well, bugger me!
Prince I will find her, never fear. No matter that it takes another hundred years of searching, you will not keep her from me, do you hear? I will not rest till I catch sight of her fair face once more. This I vow. (*Raising his sword and crying out*) AURORA!

From the bathroom there is the sound of faint cries and banging on the door

(*Listening*) What was that? Was it her? It's her! Aurora!
Carabosse Oh, I've had enough of this!
Prince (*moving off*) I'm coming my love! I'm comi —

Carabosse stabs out her hand impatiently at the Prince

Narrators (*a magic sound*) Waaaaahhhhh!

The Prince is frozen in his tracks

Second Narrator After all, what point was there in being a witch if you couldn't cheat, occasionally?
Carabosse Come here, lover.

The Prince pads over to her

Good boy! Now then, after me. (*She leads him into the song*)

This has to be love!
Prince (*as if in a trance*) This has to be love!
Both It's love at first sight, with our hearts both combining,
Our bodies will follow, our parts intertwining,
Prince My heart is for you ...
Carabosse And the rest of you, too.
Both That this really and truly,
Our passion's unruly,
This certainly has to be love!

He kisses her

Carabosse (*finally, pushing him away; speaking*) Come on, then. I'm taking you home with me!
Prince (*overjoyed*) Oh, my beloved, how wonderful.

Carabosse starts to lead the Prince out of the room. From the bathroom comes the sound of Aurora's desperate cry

Aurora (*off, calling*) Somebody, let me out of here!
Carabosse (*irritably*) Oh, I'd forgotten about her. (*Calling*) Come on, then, out you come. (*She gesticulates*)
Narrators (*another magic sound*) Waaaaahhhhh!

The offstage bathroom door flies open

Aurora spills into the room

Aurora Oh! At last! I thought I'd never — (*She breaks off as she sees them together*) Wicked godmother! Beloved? What are you both ...? Why — ?
Carabosse He's with me now, child.
Aurora You? How can he? He's my husband-to-be.
Carabosse Not any more. You've missed your chance.
Aurora I'm his future wife. Beloved, tell her you're mine. You vowed to me you were mine forever.
Carabosse Vows are made to be broken, dear.
Aurora (*tearfully*) Never!
Carabosse Ask him. Go on, ask him, then. (*To Prince*) Whose husband to be are you?

Prince Yours, beloved.
Carabosse Whose future wife am I?
Prince Mine, beloved.
Carabosse (*indicating Aurora*) Who's that, then?
Prince I've absolutely no idea. Possibly a bridesmaid?
Aurora Ooooooh .... !

She flings herself on the bed and, bursting into angry tears, drums her feet and buries her face in the pillow

Carabosse Dear! Dear! Dear! Teenage temper tantrums. You were well out of that, beloved.
Prince I should say I was, beloved.
Carabosse Come on, home time then. I promised you another chance to explore the magic forest, didn't I?
Prince Oh, jolly good!
Carabosse (*as they leave*) Ha-ha-ha-ha-ha-ha!

Carabosse and the Prince leave

The Narrators begin a sad underscore

Aurora (*in between her sobs*) ... he promised ... he made a vow ... we'd both live ... happily ... ever ... after ... he promised me ... (*She sits up*)
Second Narrator And Princess Aurora who was only sixteen — or if you count the years she'd been asleep — only a hundred and sixteen — also knew very little about men. But she was beginning to learn.
Aurora (*miserably*) I just want to go back to sleep for another hundred years ... (*She sings*)

No. 2 Aurora's Vow

That foul witch has done her worst,
This whole honeymoon is cursed.
What a tragic, sorry plight!
What's the heroine to do,
When she's trapped inside the loo?
What a horrid wedding night!
Kneeling on a freezing floor
With her ear against the door.
Knowing everything's begun,
Future husband's having fun
Whilst completely unaware
Wife-to-be's not even there.

And he didn't seem to care!
Well, let both of them, beware!

(*Speaking; more determined*) Pull yourself together, Aurora! (*She gets off the bed*)

(*Singing; more confidently*) I am nearly seventeen
And the daughter of a queen.
If it takes a thousand years,
And a waterfall of tears —
I will fight this to the death,
Till I take my final breath —
I forgot — another thing
Yes! My daddy is the king! —
I'll risk pestilence and fire
And all consequences dire.
I've an iron royal will
I am quite prepared to kill!
So wherever you may be,
I will never set him free
And you heard that first from me — so there!

At the end of the song, the bed goes

Aurora goes off

END OF PROLOGUE

ACT I

Scene 1

Carabosse's cave

A rock serving as a seat and a bed, nothing more

Third Narrator (*taking up the tale*) Carabosse, the witch, lived in a cold, damp dark cave ...

Some of the Narrators start various regular dripping noises

Narrators { Plip ... plop ... plip ... plop ... *etc.*
Drip .... drip ...... drip ... *etc.*

Third Narrator ... infested with rats and other vermin ...

The other Narrators join in with occasional scuffling, squeaking rodent sounds

Narrators { Scuffle ... scuffle ... scuffle ...
Eek ... eek ... eek ... eek ...

Third Narrator The witch's only companion, since the unfortunate death of her cat some years before, was her Familiar, the enchanted Pigcutter.

The Pigcutter enters with a besom broom. Half pig, half human, he is short, hairy and unattractive. He is at present chasing rodents swiping at them with his broom.

Pigcutter (*as he enters*) ... go on ... get out of it ... out, out ... horrible things ... Yeeurrh! Oh, these rats, they're everywhere!

From off stage, Carabosse is heard calling

Carabosse (*off, calling*) Pig! Pig! Where are you? Pig!
Pigcutter She's back! She's back!
Carabosse (*off, calling*) Pig!

Pigcutter Oh, God! Just look at the place! I haven't untidied it!
Carabosse (*off, calling*) Pig!

He throws the broom down and prepares to greet her

Carabosse enters

Pigcutter (*extending his arms to greet her*) Welcome back, mistress.
Carabosse (*ignoring him*) So this is where you're hiding, pig.
Pigcutter (*overcome*) It's so — it's so good to see —
Carabosse What have you been doing to this place while I've been away?
Pigcutter Nothing, mistress.
Carabosse It looks suspiciously to me like you've been washing the floors?
Pigcutter Me?
Carabosse You know I can't stand washed floors. What's that over there? Is that a broom? Have you been sweeping?
Pigcutter No, mistress.
Carabosse Then what's that broom doing out?
Pigcutter I — I —
Carabosse That's my best broom. Have you been sweeping up with my best broom, you horrible little porker?
Pigcutter I was only chasing rats.
Carabosse Rats?
Pigcutter There's hundreds of them. They're breeding ...
Carabosse (*romantically*) Ah! Sweet!
Pigcutter Thousands of them! If we only had a cat ...
Carabosse I had a cat.
Pigcutter He died, though.
Carabosse Whose fault's that, then, pig? (*Stabbing her finger at him twice, viciously*) Yours! Yours!
All Waaaaahhhhh! Waaaaahhhhh!
Pigcutter (*reacting, in pain*) Aaaah! Aaaah!

From a distance, the Prince's voice is heard echoing through the cave. At the sound of his voice, Carabosse's manner softens. She is clearly a woman infatuated

Prince (*off, calling*) Beloved! Where are you, beloved? I've lost you.
Carabosse (*calling back*) I'm in here, husband-to-be.
Pigcutter (*mystified*) Husband-to-be?
Prince (*off, calling*) Future wife! I can't find you!
Carabosse (*calling back*) Here, beloved! Just follow my sweet voice, beloved!

Pigcutter Future wife? Beloved? Who's this beloved, then?

Carabosse Mind your own business. I've brought home my husband-to-be. We're engaged. From now on he's living here. So, it'll be two for supper.

Pigcutter (*dismayed*) Living *here*?

The Prince enters. He wears a pair of rose-tinted spectacles

Prince (*overjoyed*) Ah! Beloved!

Carabosse (*softening immediately*) Aaaahhh!

Prince If I had lost you, my heart would have broken in two.

Carabosse I would never leave you, my darling.

Prince (*moving to her*) My beloved!

Carabosse (*holding out her arms*) My prince!

Prince (*holding her*) My little princess!

Carabosse Kiss me! Kiss me! Kiss me!

Prince Yes! Yes! Yes! (*He kisses her gently*)

Carabosse Yes! (*She kisses him deeply*)

Pigcutter (*watching this with some horror*) Oh, God, that's horrible!

Carabosse (*breaking from the embrace*) Don't look! Don't look! This is private. If I catch you staring again, I'll strike you blind!

Pigcutter (*muttering*) Fat lot of good that'll do you. Blind pig around the place.

Carabosse (*hissing*) Shut up!

Prince (*who has been looking round for the first time*) Oh! Oh! Oh! What a palace is this! Magnificent! This is magnificent, beloved!

Carabosse I'm pleased you like it, beloved.

Pigcutter He likes it?

Prince I had no idea you lived somewhere so beautiful. It must surely be enchanted!

Carabosse And if you keep those glasses on, dearest, it'll stay enchanted, I promise.

Pigcutter It's a filthy old cave!

Carabosse If you don't shut up, I'll pull your tongue out!

Pigcutter (*muttering*) Yes, that'll do it ... then you'll have a dumb pig, as well ...

Prince (*seeing the Pigcutter for the first time*) Oh-ho! Oh! Oh!

Pigcutter Eh?

Prince What a superb animal! Superb! (*Walking round the Pigcutter, inspecting him*) He must certainly be of noble pedigree?

Pigcutter (*modestly*) Well, you know ... I've been around.

Prince Where in heaven did you find this magnificent creature?

Carabosse (*muttering*) I don't know, under some stone ...

Prince Obviously of Arab stock ... head held high ... full flowing mane ... high tail ... a superb stallion, indeed ...
Pigcutter Stallion? Where'd you find this bloke?
Prince Would you permit me to ride him later, beloved?
Pigcutter Eh?
Carabosse Maybe later, beloved.
Pigcutter Yes, much later.
Carabosse Go and make us a brew.
Pigcutter A brew? What brew?
Carabosse *The* brew.
Pigcutter Oh yes, right. *The* brew. Two brews, coming up.

The Pigcutter collects the broom and shuffles off

Prince (*watching him leave, admiringly*) What a high-stepping creature! Do you ride him frequently?
Carabosse Only in emergencies.
Prince I am tempted to leap astride him. I would handle him gently, I promise.
Carabosse I'm sure.
Prince I am an accomplished rider, never fear.
Carabosse I know you are, beloved. (*Patting the rock*) Come here and sit down.

The Narrators start some romantic underscore during the next

Prince (*moving to her*) On this cosy, pure, white bed with sheets of finest silk and softest swan's down pillows ...?
Carabosse That's the one, beloved ... Am I not beautiful? Go on, tell me I'm beautiful.
Prince You're so — beautiful ... beautiful ...
Carabosse Go on ... keep saying it ...
Prince (*repeating it*) Beautiful ... beautiful ... beautiful ... beautiful ...
Carabosse That'll do ...

A love scene of sorts between them. Frustratingly for Carabosse, she has to do the work for both of them. She sings, caressing him and placing his hands where she wants them

No. 3 Do Your Worst

Now do what you once did before to me,
But this time I hope you'll do more to me.

Try taunting and teasing me, painfully pleasing me
Do your worst, do your worst!

There's acres of me worth discovering,
Whole treasures in store need uncovering
So treat me appallingly, hauling and mauling me!
Do your worst, do your worst!
This time is our chance to experiment —
Exploring our wildest dreams —
An orgy of orgasmic merriment —
First fleetingly fingering, firmly, then lingering —

Prince How's that then — ?

He starts to rub her hips vigorously

Carabosse — you've got to be teasing me
Don't scratch me and pat me, start pleasing me!
Don't bounce up and down on me like I'm some pedigree filly you want to come first!

Prince (*speaking*) Whoaa! there girl!

Carabosse Do your worst, do your worst!

Carabosse places his hands on her breasts

Put your hands there, just caressingly ...
That's good. You can soon start undressing me ...

The Prince starts to rub her breasts as if they were horse brasses in need of a shine.

Prince You like me to rub some more?
Carabosse Now they're just bloody sore!

She snatches his hands away

Don't do that!
Prince Don't do what?
Carabosse (*indignantly*) That! That! That!

She snatches his hands from her breasts and places them on her bottom

Prince You want me to rub this?
Carabosse (*wearily, losing heart*) Whatever, love
If you rub me much more, if we're clever, love
A genie will reappear, out of my fucking rear
Prince (*laughing, heartily*) Make a wish!
Carabosse How I wish! How I wish!
It's every girl's dream that a gent'll be –
Once she has got him to bed –
Keen to perform instrumentally,
First plucking or bowing her, sucking or blowing her …
Prince Are there any more ways of exciting you?
You know my life's work is delighting you.

He has a brief think. Carabosse despairs

Carabosse This love-making has to be total catastrophe.

The Prince has a sudden good idea

Prince Oh! I know! Tally-ho! Try this first! (*He makes to resume his polishing, this time between her legs*)
Carabosse This is cursed!
Prince Do my worst, do my worst!

Carabosse (*pushing him off her, furiously*) No! No! No! No! NO!

Prince (*startled*) Beloved?

Carabosse What's the matter with you?

Prince (*bewildered*) Is anything wrong, beloved?

Carabosse I want the magic back. Where's all the magic?

Prince You mean conjuring tricks, beloved?

Carabosse No, I don't mean fucking conjuring tricks! (*On the verge of tears*) You've lost all your ... all your ... it's all gone ...

Third Narrator Poor Carabosse was learning the hard way about spur of the moment love affairs.

Carabosse (*brooding*) It's me, isn't it? You don't find me beautiful any more.

Prince You're the most beautiful creature in the entire world, beloved ... beautiful ... beautiful ... beautiful ...

Carabosse You don't mean that.

Prince ... beautiful ...

Carabosse You're lying. You're just saying it.

Prince And I'll keep saying it, beloved. A thousand times if that's what you need to hear ... Beaut ——

Carabosse All right. Say it to my face then, go on. Look me straight in the eyes and say it. Go on!
Prince Very well, beloved. I will.

The Prince sits beside her on the bed again. She turns to face him. He takes off his glasses and looks at her

(*In horror*) Aaaaaaaaahhhh!

The Prince runs from the room

Carabosse glares after him then stabs her fingers viciously in the direction he has vanished

Narrators Waaaaahhhhh!
Carabosse (*furiously*) Come back here! I'm not done with you!

The Pigcutter enters from the other direction, carrying two very dirty tin mugs of dark liquid. He stares after the Prince

Pigcutter What's the matter, then? Had a little tiff?
Carabosse (*savagely*) Shut up, pig!

The Prince enters. Groping his way now, since he has a bag over his head

Prince (*muffled*) Beloved?
Carabosse Over here, beloved.
Prince (*groping his way towards her*) Beloved?
Carabosse (*taking him by the hand*) Come on then, husband-to-be, bedtime.
Prince (*relieved to feel her hand*) Oh, future wife! I thought I'd lost you.
Carabosse (*resignedly, as they go*) This way. Let's try again.
Prince (*cheerfully*) Are we going to have another go, then?

Carabosse and the Prince go off

The Pigcutter watches them

Pigcutter What makes me think that's never going to work? (*He absently takes a sip from one of the mugs and immediately regrets it. Pulling a face*) Yuuurrgghh!

The Pigcutter goes out after them. Aurora enters in a separate area

Underscore. The Lights simultaneously come up on Aurora. There is a brief inset scene

Third Narrator Several leagues away in her palace, the Princess Aurora waited sadly for her prince to return.

No. 4 Aurora's Vow (Reprise)

Aurora (*tearfully, singing*) I will wait another day,
Just in case he's lost his way.
What is taking him so long?
Though I know it's very wrong,
If he doesn't claim his wife
It will cause such utter strife
She'll be forced to take her life — so there!

Aurora bursts into tears and goes off

The Lights go down on her and we return to the cave

Carabosse returns, angry and frustrated. She paces a little, brooding

Third Narrator Carabosse was finally forced to admit that the initial fires of passion between her and the Prince had all but burnt out. The magic had gone. In her current state of frustration, unlike Princess Aurora, the witch was certainly not prepared to wait another minute. The situation called for action. And Carabosse was a woman of action.

Carabosse (*yelling*) Pig!!! Pig!!!

The Pigcutter enters hurriedly

Pigcutter Mistress?
Carabosse Fetch my fastest broom, immediately! I'm off!
Pigcutter Again, mistress?
Carabosse Go, go, go!
Pigcutter (*going off*) Yes, mistress.

The Pigcutter exits

Carabosse Yes! This calls for urgent measures! Urgent measures!

The Pigcutter returns with the broom

Pigcutter Will you be long, mistress?

Carabosse What's it to you?

Pigcutter Only I was wondering if you — if you were going to be some time whether you would possibly consider ...

Carabosse Consider what?

Pigcutter ... turning me back. Before you go.

Carabosse (*beadily*) Turning you back? What do you mean, turning you back?

Pigcutter (*babbling*) Well, I mustn't grumble — I mean, on the whole it's a great life being your Familiar and that. And then again, I get all the perks, I'm not complaining, don't get me wrong ... It's just with me being a joiner originally — (*Holding out his trotters*) — I miss the thumbs, you know ... thumbs …

The Pigcutter tails off at her expression

… thumbs.

Carabosse (*dangerously quiet*) Shut up, Pig!

Pigcutter Yes. Right. Fair enough, then.

Carabosse I'll change you back when I'm bad and ready ...

The Prince stumbles on still with the bag over his head

Prince (*muffled*) Beloved! Beloved, what's happening?

Carabosse Wait there, beloved.

Prince (*muffled*) Future wife, you're leaving?

Carabosse Won't be long.

Prince (*muffled*) Don't leave me! I cannot live without you!

Carabosse I'm just going to get some help. Professional help. For us. Back soon!

Prince (*muffled*) Don't leave me! I'll pine away and die without you!

Carabosse Oh, God! (*To the Pigcutter*) Take care of him, will you?

Pigcutter Me?

Carabosse I'll be back soooo-o-o-o-nnnnn.

Underscore

Carabosse whirls the broom round her head and with an extended cry disappears through the floor

Narrators (*as the spell works*) Waaaaahhhhh!

Prince (*as this happens, muffled*) Farewell, beloved! Farewell! Farewell! Farewell!

Slight pause

Pigcutter She's gone now. You can take the bag off, if you like.
Prince (*removing the bag, staring around him mystified*) Where am I?
Pigcutter Same place. Same old cave.
Prince What happened to the beautiful palace?
Pigcutter Ah, well. That's a long story ...
Prince Who on earth are you? You're not a stallion.
Pigcutter No. I'm a pig.
Prince What happened to the magnificent stallion?
Pigcutter He galloped off.
Prince Was she astride him? My beloved?
Pigcutter I wish.
Prince That must have been a magnificent sight. A powerful rearing beast and her, atop him! Her hair flowing ... cheeks glowing ... was that how it was?
Pigcutter Yes, all of that.
Prince (*studying him*) So. In the meantime I have you for company, do I?
Pigcutter Any problem with that?
Prince Well, you're rather grubby.
Pigcutter What do you expect, I'm a pig.
Prince Why on earth does she to allow you into her company?
Pigcutter I'm her Familiar.
Prince Familiar?
Pigcutter Yes.
Prince How familiar is familiar?
Pigcutter Well, not that familiar, unfortunately. (*Holding up his trotters again*) No thumbs, you see. Bit of a problem undoing the buttons.
Prince Her Familiar ...? How on earth did you land that job, for heaven's sake?

No. 5 Particular

Pigcutter
I'm not particular, not that particular,
If you stand me in a crowd I'm hard to see,
But for someone who's not specially particular
She's especially particular to me.

If I hadn't been out on this job on this particular day
And I hadn't turned off on this path, down this particular way,
And at this particular moment, I hadn't just chanced to see,

At this particular point in time, this tall particular tree.
And I didn't particul'ly notice this moment in time was sat
On this particular topmost branch was this particular cat.
If I hadn't particul'ly chopped on that particular side,
It would never have flattened the cat which probably wouldn't have died.

I'm not particular, not that particular,
If you stand me in a crowd I'm hard to see,
But for someone who's not specially particular
She's especially particular to me.

At that very particular time, she'd not come wandering by
Then she'd not've particul'ly yelled at this particular guy
She would never have gone and cursed him, before they'd a chance to chat.

How's he particul'ly meant to know it's her particular cat?
If that particular twist of fortune had never occurred to me
I prob'ly never have met her, gone home and had my tea.
At first I wasn't too happy, particul'ly keen to stay
Then somehow she captures your heart, in her own particular way.

I'm not particular, not that particular,
If you stand me in a crowd I'm hard to see,
But for someone who's not specially particular
She's especially particular to me —
She's especially particular to me.

A silence between them

Prince (*at length, impressed*) Well. That's a heck of a tale, that is.
Pigcutter As the prince said to the pig. (*He laughs*)
Prince (*laughing, then looking puzzled*) Sorry? No, I don't get that ...
Pigcutter Never mind. I must get on. Can't hang around here.

Prince Can I help at all?
Pigcutter Oh. Ta. I could do with a hand.
Prince (*laughing*) As the pig said to the prince. (*As they go off*) Did you get that? Hand, you see?
Pigcutter (*rather dourly*) Yes, I got that.

The Pigcutter and the Prince go off

Underscore. Under the next the Lights fade and the scene changes

Fifth Narrator And while the prince and the pigcutter both stayed, in their respective ways, under the witch's spell, Carabosse herself arrived in a trice thanks to her fastest broomstick, at the Grand Hall of Sorcerers for an audience with the Supreme Sorceress herself.

Scene 2

The Grand Hall of Sorcerers

Another cavern. We get an impression that it is very large indeed. A pronounced echo

Carabosse pops up through the floor with her broomstick

There is an eerie moaning sound, like a distant wind down a long corridor

Carabosse (*arriving*) Hah! (*Looking around her*) Yes! (*Calling*) Hallo! Hallo! Anyone at home? Hallo!
Narrators (*a whispered echo, growing increasingly fainter*) Hallo ... hallo ... hallo ... hallo ...
Carabosse Anyone at home?
Narrators (*a whispered echo, growing increasingly fainter*) Home ... home ... home ... home ...?
Carabosse I hate this place. It gives me the creeps ...
Narrators (*a whispered echo, growing increasingly fainter*) Creeps ... creeps ... creeps ... creeps ...
Carabosse It's me Carabosse!
Narrators (*a whispered echo, growing increasingly fainter*) Carabosse ... Carabosse ... Carabosse ... Carabosse ...
Fifth Narrator And as she waited there, Carabosse started to get a little nervous, suddenly. Was this, she asked herself, such a good idea after all? But it was too late to turn back now ...

Narrators Waaaaahhhhh!

The Supreme Sorceress appears and stands, almost invisible, in the shadows

Sorceress (*genially*) Good evening, Carabosse.

Carabosse (*startled*) Oh! Your evil wickedness, good morning.

Sorceress No, good *evening*, Carabosse. Here it is invariably night-time, you should know that.

Carabosse Oh, yes, I'm so sorry your imperial viciousness ...

Sorceress And to what do we owe this pleasure, Carabosse, after all these years?

Carabosse Well, your vile, sadistic, corruptness, you see —

Sorceress We can drop the polite formalities, Carabosse. Supreme Mistress, if you must.

Carabosse Thank you, Supreme Mistress.

Sorceress Tell me, now, what have you been up to, since I last saw you? A hundred and seventeen years ago, was it? How time flies. So?

Carabosse (*flustered*) Well, I've been – er ... I've been ... nothing to speak of ...

Sorceress Apart from putting innocent princesses to sleep for a hundred years?

Carabosse (*laughing nervously*) Oh, yes, I'm sorry, I forgot about that. I —

Sorceress You don't need to apologize, that was excellent, Carabosse, excellent. Beautifully done ... The spindle was an inspired touch.

Carabosse Thank you, Supreme Mistress, thank you —

Sorceress Now, I haven't much time. Come, the reason for your visit?

Fifth Narrator But Carabosse was beginning to lose her nerve. How was she to confess to the Supreme Sorceress that she, Carabosse, a fully fledged witch, had fallen in love?

Carabosse I – er – I've – er done something – rather – well, Supreme Mistress, it's a little complicated ... I – er ... don't know how to put it, really – er – it's a long, long story —

Sorceress Oh, Carabosse, I so detest long, long stories. When someone starts on a long, long story I always suspect them of telling me a short, short, short story whilst trying to avoid coming to the point.

Carabosse It's a little complicated ...

Sorceress If it's that complicated then I insist that we both sit down, Carabosse. Here ...

The Sorceress gestures. Two seats emerge from the floor

Narrators Woooooohhhhh!

One of the chairs has long vicious-looking metal spikes sticking out of its seat. The Sorceress sits on the other normal chair

Sorceress Please. Do take the visitors' chair. You'll find it serves to jog the memory.

Carabosse (*eyeing the chair*) No, no, no, thank you. It's just — er ... well I feel a little foolish in a way — I've done something — I've done something ——

Sorceress You've done something — what?

Carabosse I've fallen — er — I've fallen in — I know one's not supposed to as a — as a witch — but I've ——

Sorceress If you continue like this, I'm going to have to insist you sit down, Carabosse ...

Carabosse No, thank you, Supreme Mistress, I ...

Sorceress ... unless you come to the point at once and stop wasting my time. Now, either speak up or sit down, Carabosse, one or the other!

Carabosse whimpers

Carabosse (*taking a deep breath, rapidly*) I've fallen in love with a handsome prince and I don't know what to do.

Slight pause

Sorceress I see.

Carabosse Are you shocked?

Sorceress No, I'm not shocked. I already knew.

Carabosse Oh. Well, then ...

Sorceress I'm not shocked, Carabosse, I'm disappointed. You have been extremely stupid, weak-willed and have indulged in behaviour totally unbecoming to a witch. You have brought shame on our entire coven ...

Carabosse I didn't — I couldn't ——

Sorceress (*sharply*) And if you continue to interrupt me, I warn you I will compel you to sit down, Carabosse ——

Slight pause. Underscore from the Narrators

(*More calmly*) Let me tell you something. I am considerably older than you and I have, as they say, been round the block a few times. In fact, in most cases I was there before it was built. The first thing I need to tell you is that you are not in love.

Carabosse I — I'm sure ——

Sorceress (*snapping*) Be quiet! I hate to break it to you, Carabosse, but what you are undergoing at present is lust. Plain old, common or garden lust. Which, whilst perfectly healthy in a woman of your age, is never, ever to be confused with love. Which is altogether different and far less healthy in a woman of your age. Now, Carabosse, the thing to remember ... (*She sings*)

No.6 Love Comes Later

Lust doesn't last.
It's the rocket nature uses at the launch of an affair,
That propels you into orbit till you're weightless in the air,
Defying earth's gravity,
Delicious depravity!
But there's a further consequence on which you can depend,
Inevitably what goes up is destined to descend.
Lust doesn't last.
And once the passion crashes and infatuation cools.
Often, sifting through the ashes, you will see two sorry fools,
Both watching the embers die,
But neither remembers why —
Just what it was that took them to the heights of such desire,
Whatever happened to the spark which started all that fire?
No, lust doesn't last.

Love comes later.

When they sift through the debris,
On occasions they will see,
What at first appears to be
A tiny jewel.

If they hold it to the light,
They will sometimes catch the sight
Of a phoenix in full flight
Of renewal.

And soon they'll be flying

Their feet off the ground,
The whole of the world beneath them
Both cloud cuckoo bound

But that, my dear, is love.
And love comes, later.
Real love, true love,
Comes much, much, oh so much, later ...

Carabosse That's all very well. Lust or love, love or lust, I'm desperate. I must have him. I must. You haven't told me what I want to know, Supreme Mistress.

Sorceress (*impatiently*) Then what is it you do want to know, you stupid creature?

Carabosse How to win him. I need to know how to win him. How to win his heart.

Sorceress Well, that's simple enough! He's a man, isn't he? He's a half witted, one track, typically human male. How do you think you do it?

Carabosse I don't know. Tell me!

Sorceress You've stooped to the level of mere mortals, so if you want to win this wretched animal's heart, you will have to do it the way a plain, powerless mortal female does.

Carabosse How?

Sorceress I don't know. I'm not a mortal, am I? Whatever mortal women do to win their men. Primp and preen. Wiggle and jiggle. Woo him, flatter him, seduce him. In the last resort, feed the brute, fill his vacuous face with food. Whatever it takes to persuade the idiot he's in love with you.

Carabosse He can't bear the sight of me. He runs away whenever I ...

Sorceress Then I should smarten yourself up, girl. Have a — whatever mortal women call it — a hair-do.

Carabosse (*mystified*) A hair-do?

Sorceress Oh, go away, Carabosse, stop wasting my time. Get out of my sight, you pathetic, snivelling creature.

Carabosse I — I —

Sorceress (*fiercely, pointing*) *Go!* Before I make you sit down there for a hundred years, until every scrap of lust has left you!

Carabosse (*meekly*) Yes, Supreme Mistress. (*She turns unhappily and makes to leave the room, trailing her broom*)

Sorceress And Carabosse ... You won't require the broomstick.

Carabosse But I need it to get home ...

Sorceress You will find it no longer works for you. Not as a means of transport. You can leave it here with me. I have decided, Carabosse, to withdraw all your powers, until further notice.

Carabosse (*shocked*) Oh!

Sorceress If you've chosen to behave like a mortal, then you will have to live as a mortal. No more spells, no more broomstick rides for you ...

Carabosse (*meekly*) How am I to get home?

Sorceress You walk, dear. Like the rest of your kind.

Carabosse How long is this going to last?

Sorceress Until you finally come to your senses and realize the extent of your folly. Or until your heart is broken. Whichever is the sooner.

Carabosse My heart's already broken.

Sorceress I rather doubt it, you know, Carabosse. I doubt it.

With a flourish, the Sorceress withdraws Carabosse's powers

Narrators Waaaaahhhhh!

Carabosse is whirled round briefly, as the force of the spell catches her. She cries out

Carabosse Aaaaahhhhh!

The Sorceress goes out swiftly

The crestfallen Carabosse is alone

A brief inset scene

A light comes up on the Pigcutter who comes hurrying on, startled

Pigcutter What the hell was that?

Prince (*off, alarmed*) Oh, no! No! No!

The Prince appears briefly in the doorway

(*Agitatedly*) The spell is lifted! The Princess. I must go to the Princess.

The Prince rushes off

(*Shouting as he goes*) Aurora! Aurora!

Pigcutter (*leaving*) Oy! Where do you think you're going? I'm supposed to keep an eye on you. Now I'm in the doghouse.

The Pigcutter exits

Fifth Narrator And Carabosse, stripped of all her powers, no longer a witch, reduced to the status of a mere mortal began her long trudge home.

Carabosse leaves

Scene 3

The grounds of Princess Aurora's castle

Sixth Narrator The Prince though, freed from the witch's spell and being a natural athlete made altogether faster progress to be reunited with his original true love. And only just in time, for the Princess Aurora had lost hope of ever seeing her husband-to-be again.

Aurora wanders on disconsolately

The sun shines. A solitary bird starts to sing

First Narrator (*a repetitive call*) Tweet-tweet-tweet-tweet! Tweet-tweet-tweet-tweet! Tweet-tweet-tweet-tweet! (*Etc.*)

Aurora (*softly*) Oh, tiny bird! If you knew how unhappy I am, you would not sing so sweetly. There surely is no song in the whole wide world which can mend my broken heart. I will sit here by the lake, tie both my shoelaces together and then jump in and drown myself.

Second Narrator (*joining the first*) Quack! Quack, quack, quack! Quack! Quack, quack, quack! (*Etc.*)

Aurora (*sitting on the ground*) Yes, Mr Duck. Be patient! I will join you in the deep water and swim with you for a while until my strength is exhausted. (*She starts to untie her shoe laces*)

Third Narrator (*joining the chorus*) Cuck – oo! Cuck – oo! Cuck – oo! Cuck – oo! (*Etc.*)

Aurora Oh, Mrs Cuckoo! Have you come to say farewell to me?

Fourth Narrator (*joining the increasingly noisy chorus*) Ribbit! Ribbit! Ribbit! (*Etc.*)

Aurora (*raising her voice slightly*) Wait! Wait, Mr Frog! I'm coming! Don't be so impatient!

Fifth Narrator (*joining the hubbub*) Moooo! Moooo! Moooo! (*Etc.*)

She is now tying both sets of her shoelaces together. The animal sounds have combined into a sort of musical fugue

Aurora (*shouting*) Oh, look! Even the cows have come to moo me goodbye! Farewell, dear friendly cows!

Sixth Narrator (*joining in finally to the deafening din*) Eee-aww! Eee-aww! (*Etc.*)

Aurora (*yelling above the pandemonium*) Dearest old Donkey! Goodbye! Goodbye! (*Standing, screaming*) All right! All right! I'm coming! Don't be so impatient!

At this point the Prince enters, breathless from running. He takes in the scene

The fugue has reached a climax

Prince (*shouting to her above the noise*) Aurora! Aurora! *Aurora!* (*Clapping his hands*) Quietly! Quietly, please! Would you all please *be quiet*!!!

Silence

The Narrators, startled, disperse

All (*variously, as they depart*) Tweet-tweet-tweet-tweet! Quack! Quack, quack, quack! Cuck – oo! Cuck – oo! Cuck – oo! Cuck – oo! Ribbit! Ribbit! Ribbit! Moooo! Moooo! Moooo! Eee-aww! Eee-aww! (*Etc.*)

The Narrators exit

Prince That's better.

Aurora (*turning, with difficulty, to see him*) Oh! Husband-to-be!

Prince (*extending his arms to her*) Future wife!

Aurora Oh, my love, you've returned! (*She starts to run to him but, after a pace, falls on her face*) Oh!

Prince (*springing forward, concerned*) Beloved! (*He kneels by her*) What is the matter?

Aurora My shoelaces, I forgot — they were ——

Prince (*laughing*) Why, they are tied together! (*He laughs*)

Aurora Why, so they are ... ! (*She laughs*)

Prince (*smiling and stroking her cheek*) You foolish thing! No wonder!

Aurora (*smiling*) No wonder!

They laugh some more together

But, you've returned to me, future husband! You've returned!

Prince (*starting to retie her laces*) As soon as I could, wife-to-be, as soon as I escaped the witch's wicked spell. (*Pausing in his task, overcome by a sudden burst of love*) Oh, such sweet, petite feet! (*He kisses them*)

Aurora Oh! My love! Never leave me again!

Prince I swear upon my uncle's — no, he's dead — my other uncle's life.

Aurora Stay with me forever!

Prince So long as I have breath to breathe.

He takes a deep breath and pulls her to her feet

Now, beloved, we must flee. For I fear the witch is pursuing me and is, even now, not far behind.

Aurora Oh!

Prince The first place she will come will be here to your palace. We must fly somewhere else.

Aurora I don't know somewhere else. I've never been there.

Prince To the City.

Aurora The City?

Prince I was there once on a quest. We shall be safe in the City. It is big enough to hide us. She will never find us there.

Aurora But I could not live in the City. Amidst other people. (*She shudders*)

Prince Well. The Suburbs, then. There are slightly fewer people there. We will live in the Suburbs.

Aurora The Suburbs? Where are they?

Prince Oh, you will adore them. We will buy a small cottage, just the two of us, and live in the Suburbs.

Aurora How small a cottage?

Prince Oh, tiny.

Aurora What about the children?

Prince Children?

Aurora Where will our children live? If our cottage is so tiny ...

Prince Oh. Well, it needn't be that tiny. It can be quite a big cottage.

Aurora My darling, have we the money to buy this?

Prince Oh, yes. I have gold in my purse here.

Aurora How much gold?

Prince (*getting a bit impatient with all this*) Enough! Enough! And if there isn't enough gold, why then I can sell my crown ...

Aurora Yes, and I can sell my crown. And, if need be, my rings and jewels ...

Prince And if necessary my trusty sword!

Aurora Oh no, not your trusty sword. You must never sell your trusty sword!
Prince We shall see! We shall see! Are you ready?
Aurora Oh, yes.
Prince This is exciting!
Aurora What an adventure!
Prince Come my love!
Aurora Off we go!

They start to go off, together

How many children shall we have, do you think?
Prince (*uncertainly*) Well, I think we'll have to wait and see. How many do you want?
Aurora Oh, masses and masses. Millions! As many as possible!
Prince Ah. Good-o.

They both go

Scene 4

Carabosse's cave

First Narrator After days of walking, Carabosse finally arrived back home.

Carabosse limps on, exhausted

Carabosse (*hoarsely, calling*) Pig!! Pig!! Help me!

The Pigcutter rushes on and sees her

Pigcutter Mistress! Oh, mistress ...

She sways and he hurries forward to support her

Here, allow me ...

He helps her to the rock and sits her down. He continues to hold her

I've been really worried about you. I had this feeling something was wrong. I suppose it was being your Familiar. I don't mind saying, mistress, if anything happened to you ... I don't know what I'd ... I really don't ...

Carabosse (*recovering*) All right that'll do! That'll do! Don't clutch on to me like that!

Pigcutter Sorry.

Carabosse Everything been all right here whilst I've been gone?

Pigcutter Er — well. You want the bad news or the bad news?

Carabosse Tell me the worst.

Pigcutter He's gone. Your beloved's run off. Couple of days ago, he ran off shouting the Princess's name, Aurora! Aurora! As if he'd just remembered it, all of a sudden. Like the spell had been lifted.

Carabosse It had. I've lost all my powers, pig.

Pigcutter What?

Carabosse They've been taken away.

Pigcutter How do you know?

Carabosse There! (*She stabs her fingers at him*) Feel anything?

Pigcutter Nothing.

Carabosse There you are, then.

Pigcutter Are you sure?

Carabosse Would I have walked all the way back here, otherwise? I need to get organized. Quickly, my crock of gold! I need that.

Pigcutter What all of it?

Carabosse The whole lot.

Pigcutter I thought you said you were saving that for a rainy day.

Carabosse Listen, pig, at this stage of my life, it's pissing down. Now fetch that gold!

Pigcutter Yes, mistress.

The Pigcutter goes off

Carabosse (*briefly alone*) Now, how did she put it ... ? Primp and preen, what's that? (*She primps and preens*) What's primping, then? Oh, I don't know how to primp. I've never primped in my life ... Wiggle and jiggle. Try that. (*She wiggles and jiggles*)

The Pigcutter enters with her sack of gold. He watches her mystified

Listen, you're a man ...

Pigcutter No I'm not. I'm a pig. No spell lifted here, I notice.

Carabosse No. That's peculiar. I wonder why that is. Perhaps it's because it's a curse. Yes, I remember now, I cursed you. I never cast a spell. I was too angry.

Pigcutter I recall.

Carabosse But you were a man.

Pigcutter Used to be once.

Carabosse So ... (*She wiggles and jiggles*) ... What does this do for you? As a man?

Pigcutter Well, I have to say, speaking as an ex-man, currently a pig ... not a lot. (*He watches her for a second*)

Carabosse (*impatiently, wiggling*) No! As a man? As a man?

Pigcutter Give us a clue, then. What's it supposed to do?

Carabosse (*giving up*) I don't bloody know. Drive you mad with desire, something like that?

Pigcutter (*catching on, humouring her, rather unconvincingly*) Oh, yes. Yeah! Yeah! 'Cor — fancy a bit of that. Phwhooaarr! Whey-hey-hey! (*He growls*)

Carabosse It does nothing for you, does it?

Pigcutter It could maybe grow on me.

Carabosse Yes, like mildew on a dead bat. Right, I'm off. Give me that!

Pigcutter (*alarmed, giving her the bag*) Now?

Carabosse I need to get him back. He's with her, I know he is. That spoilt little bitch of a princess. He doesn't want her. He needs a real woman. Once he's been with a real woman, he'll forget all about her.

Pigcutter Where are you going?

Carabosse To the City. That's full of real women. I'll soon pick it up, don't worry. I'll be primping and preening, jiggling and wiggling with the best of them. When I come back, he'll be running after me, begging for it, you'll see. You'll see!

She starts to leave with her bag

(*In the doorway*) And maybe I'll even learn to cook!

She leaves with a flourish

The Pigcutter stands dumbfounded

Pigcutter (*to himself*) Not roast pork, I hope.

Underscore as the Lights change for the next scene

Scene 5

A street somewhere in the Big City

No. 7 Busy in the City

Narrators It's busy, busy, busy in the city.
Busy city, busy city, busy city,
Beep-beep! vroom-vroom! crash-bang! shout-shout!
Yeehaw, yeehaw! paarrpp-paarrrp! look out!

The underscore continues under the following

The Prince and Aurora enter, hand in hand. She, in particular, is very awed by their surroundings. The Prince, though equally so, is trying to look cool. A Woman on her mobile passes by them

Woman 1 ... no, our Tracy's such big thighs ...
Didn't have one in her size ...

Aurora I'm getting very tired, you know, from all this walking. I've never walked so far in my whole life.

A Man on his mobile passes them

Man 1 ... caught them at it in his bed ...
Poor old Colin, just dropped dead ...

Prince Don't worry, we'll soon be there.
Aurora (*as they wander into the road*) We'll soon be where?
Narrators (*a motor horn*) Beeeeeeep!

They both jump

Prince I wish they wouldn't keep doing that. (*Shouting after the car*) That's extremely irritating, you know!

Another Woman on her mobile passes them

Woman 2 ... hallo, darling, me again ...
I'm just running for the train ...

Prince (*looking around*) Now, let's see ...

Aurora What are we looking for, exactly? Are we looking for a house?
Prince No. We're — looking for a shop that sells houses.
Aurora That sells big houses.
Prince Fairly big houses.

Another Man on his mobile passes them

Man 2 ... sell the lot, that's my advice ...
Chance like this won't happen twice! ...

Prince (*seeing somewhere across the road*) Aha! What's that place over there? That looks likely.

Another Woman on her mobile passes them

Woman 3 ... she found out that he was gay ...
Had to happen to poor Fay ...

Prince Come on, beloved! I think it's going to rain.
Aurora Oh, no!

He leads her across the road evidently straight into the path of traffic

Narrators (*various horns*) Beeep! Baaarrrp! Boop-boop! Weeeewaah! Weeewah!
Prince (*irritably*) Oh, do stop that!
Aurora (*shrilly*) Go away! Go away! (*She glares at the traffic and stamps her foot*)

Another Man on his mobile passes them

Man 3 ... laser disk and mini-cam ...
Thirty gigabytes of ram ...

Prince Come on, beloved. Hurry up, or you'll get wet.
Aurora Oh, no ...

The Prince and Aurora go off

During the following, Carabosse comes on from another direction, carrying her bag of gold

Narrators It's hustle, bustle-bustle in the city,
Busy city, busy city, busy city,
Stand back! Keep clear! Watch out! Hey, you!
Hal-lo! Good-day! Coo-eee! Woo-hoo!

Carabosse Ah! Nothing like the Big City. Smell that pollution. Now ... where next?

Narraators (*thunder noises*) Ruuummmble! Ruuummmble! Ruuummmble!

Carabosse (*glaring at the sky*) Oh, bugger it!

Another Woman on her mobile passes

Woman 4 ... well, it took her unawares ...
Had to have it on the stairs ...

Carabosse (*vainly, after Woman 4*) I say, excuse me!

Another Man on his mobile passes

Man 4 ... yes, well ... yes, well ... yes, well, true ...
Listen, would I lie to you?

Carabosse (*vainly, after Man 4*) ... excuse me!

Another Woman on her mobile passes

Woman 5 ... no, I ... no, I ... yes, I heard ....
Promise, sweetie, not one word ...

Carabosse (*vainly*) I say! ... What's the matter with these people ...?

Another Man on his mobile passes

Man 5 ... look, I've changed my mind, instead,
Fourteen cases of the red ...

Carabosse Oy! (*She points her fingers frustratedly after Man 5, trying to cast a spell, but to no avail*) Useless!

Narrators (*louder thunder noises*) Ruuummmble! Ruuummmble! Ruuummmble!

Carabosse stares up at the sky

Another Woman on her mobile passes

Woman 6 ... I was simply hopping mad ...
Only decent one I had ...

Carabosse (*stepping into the woman's path*) Oy, you!
Woman 6 (*startled*) I beg your pardon?
Carabosse I'm looking for a hair-do ...
Woman 6 A what?
Carabosse A hair-do!
Woman 6 (*still not understanding her*) Sorry?
Carabosse (*shouting at her*) A hair .... do! A place that does your hair. (*To herself*) Just my luck to pick a bloody foreigner ...
Woman 6 Oh, you mean a hairdressers? There's a frightfully good salon just along there.
Carabosse Along there, you say?
Woman 6 They do just about everything. But they're frightfully exclusive. You'll need an appointment.
Carabosse I've no time for that. This is an emergency! (*She starts to move away*)
Woman 6 Yes, I can tell it is. (*Going back to her phone, as she goes*) Hallo, darling, sorry about that. I just got stopped by this dreadful scarecrow ...
Carabosse (*hearing this*) What did you call me? (*She angrily stabs her fingers after the woman, again to no effect*) Oh! Oh, to strike someone dead!
Narrators (*very loud thunder noises*) Ruuummmble! Ruuummmble! Ruuummmble!

Carabosse stares up at the sky again

And down came the rain! Sssssshhhhhhhsssshhhh! Plippp! Plipp! (*Etc.*)
Carabosse Oh, sod it!

Carabosse rushes off during the next dodging the traffic, avoiding the rain

Narrators It's muscle tussle-tussle in the city,
Busy city, busy city, busy city,
Don't cross, one way, look left, cross now!
You fool! My God! Look out! Daft cow!

Scene 6

An Estate Agent's office

Aurora and the Prince are sitting on two chairs in the reception area. Both have got rather wet since we last saw them. Something has happened to the bright colour in their clothes. Where the rain has caught it, the fabric has faded to patches of grey

Aurora How long do we have to wait, here?
Prince He said he'll be with us, right this moment.
Aurora I've got extremely wet.
Prince So have I.
Aurora I'm very uncomfortable.
Prince So am I.
Aurora My dress is all ... (*Examining her clothing more closely*) Oh!
Prince What's the matter?
Aurora The colour's faded. This rain's taken all the colour.
Prince Really?
Aurora Look, it's the same with you. Your lovely jacket's spoilt. Completely ruined. We need new clothes now, as well.
Prince (*rather anxiously*) Yes, first things first, beloved.
Aurora I can't wear this any more, can I?
Prince Yes, yes. It's just — er — well, I think we might have to be a little careful with money to start with, future wife ... just till we've found out how much the house will cost.
Aurora We have all your gold, don't we?
Prince Yes.
Aurora That should surely be enough?
Prince I hope so. But I've been looking at the house prices in the display case over there. I just hope we've — er — brought enough.
Aurora Surely we have. As we said, there's my crown. And then there's your crown. And there's my jewels. And in the very last resort, there's always your trusty sword. That should be enough, surely. (*Making to remove her crown*) Why, this crown alone cost my good fairy godmother an absolute ... Oh! What's happened to it? It's paper. It's turned to paper. Look! (*She bends and twists it*)
Prince Oh. That's curious.
Aurora (*her hands flying to her neck*) My jewels, they're all — look at them ... (*She tears off her necklace and throws it down*) Just look! Look at that! My rings, as well. They're all ruined. Now I'm going to need new jewels, aren't I?
Prince (*slowly removing his crown, thoughtfully*) Yes, yes ...

Aurora Husband-to-be, what's happening? Everything's melting away ... crumbling like ...

Prince Yes, I — I can only think — I can only theorize ... that in this normal world — things behave — differently. Apparently.

Aurora What about your trusty sword?

Prince Oh yes, I'm sure I can rely on my trusty ... (*He makes to draw it from its scabbard. There is a handle to it, but no blade*) Ah!

Aurora Oh. (*In a panic*) You still have the gold? Your gold hasn't …?

The Prince anxiously opens his purse

Prince (*relieved*) Yes, it's all here, thank heavens ... Yes .... (*He stares at the purse's contents and frowns*)

Aurora (*anxiously*) What's wrong?

Prince Well, as I say, I'm not altogether certain whether we're going to have — quite enough ——

Aurora For another trusty sword?

He is silent

For jewels?

He is silent

For fresh crowns?

He is silent

For new clothes?

He is silent

Not even for a house?

Prince Maybe — a — a very, very small flat.

Aurora (*mystified*) A *flat*? What on earth is a flat?

The Estate Agent enters

Agent So sorry to keep you, sir, madam. I've not been wasting your precious time, though, I promise you that. I've just been sorting out a few initial properties to show you. Just to give us an idea of what you're both looking for. Now, you did specify something on the large side, didn't you? ... If you'd both care to follow me ...?

Aurora and the Prince rise, rather sheepishly

(*Leading them both off, laughing*) ... walk this way ... Now as I say, of course it rather depends on what you mean by large, precisely ...

Prince Yes. I suppose it does rather ...

They go out

The Lights change to another brief inset scene: outside the mouth of the cave

The Pigcutter comes on carrying a plank of wood, obviously in the middle of building something

Narrators (*very loud thunder noises*) Ruuummmble! Ruuummmble! Ruuummmble!

Pigcutter (*anxiously staring at the sky*) I hope she'll be all right in all this. She's not very fond of water.

After a second the Pigcutter goes in again

The Lights fade

Scene 7

A similar reception area of a rather grand hairdressing salon and beauty clinic

Carabosse is standing, waiting impatiently with her bag

Suitable underscore. A silent sequence

Sixth Narrator Just round the corner in Mr De Vine's Hairdressing and Beauty Salon, Carabosse was also being kept waiting, although in her case, with considerably less patience.

An Assistant, wearing a pink smock, comes hurrying on. She stops in alarm when she sees Carabosse

(*During the following*) It seemed as if the salon was reluctant to accept Carabosse. After all, it did cater to the most exclusive and elegant clientele.

The Assistant and Carabosse have an inaudible conversation where Carabosse points to her head, miming. The Assistant declines pointing first to her watch and then indicating that the salon is fully booked, finally that they are closed. Carabosse starts to yell at her. The Assistant tries to quieten her but Carabosse obviously refuses to be quietened. The Assistant attempts to usher Carabosse towards the street door but the latter resists. The two of them start pushing and shoving and appear to be on the verge of coming to blows

The Beauty Manager enters. He is also dressed in pink. He tries to intercede between the two of them, also asking Carabosse to leave

Carabosse argues with both of them pointing to her hair. The other two shake their heads in refusal. Carabosse is finally on the verge of being pushed out into the street. The Manager takes up Carabosse's bag which had been put down in the kerfuffle. He is startled by its weight. Carabosse tries to snatch the bag back from the Manager. The Assistant joins in. The three have a brief tussle with the bag during the following

But the important thing about Mr De Vine's salon was not only did its clients need to be exclusive and elegant, they also had to be very, very, very *rich*.

At this point, the contents of the bag, a number of gold bars, spill out on to the floor. The Manager and the Assistant's manner alters abruptly. The Manager dispatches the assistant to fetch someone

The Assistant exits

Meanwhile, with a sycophantic, apologetic smile the Manager helps Carabosse re-load her bag

And, suddenly, here was a client rich enough to merit the full and undivided attention of Mr De Vine himself.

Immediately, Mr De Vine enters holding both hands out ingratiatingly to Carabosse

No. 8 Welcome

De Vine Madam! Welcome!
Welcome! Welcome! Welcome!
Yes, there's so much we can do

And we promise when we're through,
We'll have made a perfect woman out of you!

Two Beauticians step forward

I'd like you to meet first our secret magicians
Our qualified, certified team of beauticians.

Beauticians Madam! Welcome!
Welcome! welcome! welcome!
We'll shine your teeth and clean your blood,
We'll cover you in cleansing mud,
We'll set your colon in full flood.
We'll shape your brows, debag your eyes,
Each wart and birthmark we'll disguise
Exfoliate between your thighs.
We'll bleach your skin, provide a pair
Of pants to lift your derrière,
(They're undetectable in wear).
We'll recommend a wonder bra
That gets you worshipped from afar
And makes you feel a movie star,
We'll help select your outer wear,
Cool daytime chic, hot nightime bare
Just watch the paparazzi stare –
Click! Flash! Snap!
Yes, there's so much we can do
And we promise when we're through,
We'll have made a perfect woman out of you!

Three Hairdressers step forward

De Vine And next, introducing our hairdressing team,
Here to create you a stylistic dream.

Hairdressers Madam! Welcome!
Welcome! Welcome! Welcome!
We'll fashion your locks till you look like a queen
All bouncing and glowing with natural sheen.
As Samson's Delilah was fully aware,
The power of a person resides in the hair.
Appearance is vital for women today,
In bedroom or boardroom, or simply at play.
To this present style are you deeply attached?

The choice seems to cut it or have it all thatched.
It's never been washed, it has shocking split ends,
And, dear lord above! — simply swarming with friends ...
We'll alter your shade with a wave of our wand —
From brunette to auburn or redhead to blonde —
The choices are endless, feel free to select.
But first we will wash it and then disinfect.

Yes, there's so much we can do
And we promise when we're through,
We'll have made a perfect woman out of you

De Vine Madam! Madam! Madam! Madam! Madam!

A couch arises. De Vine takes Carabosse by the hand and eventually lies her down

But finally it's down to me.
Transforming you cosmetic'lly
A man with magic surgeon's hands
Who women's bodies understands.
I promise nothing drastic
A little touch of plastic,
Your skin like taut elastic
Your body more gymnastic
I'll make you look fantastic.
A dietary correction,
A carefully placed injection,
To cause benign infection —
Judicious protein filling
To make your lips look thrilling,
Accessible and willing!
I can strip you, I can snip you
I can rip you and re-zip you,
I can nip it, I can tuck it
I can lipo, I can suck it
Drain it all into a bucket.
I can carve you, I can halve you,
I can staple, stitch and starve you.
Perfect breasts, full size, high flown
In heaving, life-like silicone,
No one will guess they're not your own!

Yes, there's so much I can do,

And I promise when I'm through,
I'll have made a perfect woman out of you!

All Yes, there's so much that we can do
And we promise when we're through,
We'll have made a perfect woman —
— Made a perfect woman —
— We'll have made a perfect woman out of you!

The song concludes

Carabosse descends on the couch and disappears from view

Carabosse (*as she goes with a cry*) MAGIC!!!! (*She gives another of her discordant cackling laughs*)

Black-out

End of Act I

ACT II

Entr'acte

Scene 1

The same bare stage

The Narrators assemble

Narrators And in the months that followed:—

Aurora and the Prince enter happily hand in hand

First Narrator The Prince and Princess had quietly got married —
Second Narrator — and now wished to be known as plain Mr and Mrs Prince —
Aurora (*smiling happily*) I changed my name to his.

Aurora and the Prince leave

Third Narrator — and currently lived in a two room flat at number 29 Brown Brick Road —
Fourth Narrator — which was very pleasant for a first home —
Fifth Narrator — for which they had managed to obtain a reasonable mortgage —
Sixth Narrator — thanks to the fact that they both found jobs —
First Narrator — Mr Prince working as a supermarket shelf stacker — with every prospect of swift promotion —

A quick burst of jolly supermarket underscore

The Prince enters and crosses with a case of marmalade

Prince (*as he goes, cheerily*) Who was it now, looking for marmalade?

The Prince exits

First Narrator — for which he was fairly well-paid —

Fourth and Fifth Narrators Crash!!!
Prince (*off*) Whoops!
Second and Third Narrators Tinkle tinkle!
First Narrator — less breakages.
Second Narrator Whilst Aurora had found a job as a waitress in a topless bar for which, including hidden extras, she was very well paid indeed —

A burst of more sultry music

Aurora enters and crosses, apparently topless but concealing her breasts with a tray load of iced lagers

Aurora (*as she does this*) Brrrh! Chilly!

Aurora exits

The Prince returns

Prince — rather *over* paid, if you ask me —
Third Narrator — but then Mr Prince had little or no idea of what his wife's job entailed —
Fourth Narrator — presuming that a topless bar was a bar without a roof —
Fifth Narrator — which probably explained why Mrs Prince came home exhausted and often extremely chilly —
Sixth Narrator — but she would never take Mr Prince's advice and take her extra woolly jumper to work —
Prince (*shaking his head*) Women!
First Narrator Still, she was getting plenty of fresh air and that had to be healthy —
Second Narrator — which was just as well because very soon —
Third Narrator — in a few days from now —
Fourth Narrator — Mrs Prince was going to have to stop work altogether —
Fifth Narrator — and it was important she was fighting fit —
Sixth Narrator — for at number 29 Brown Brick Road, there was about to occur —
Narrators A happy event!

Aurora returns and runs to the Prince

Sixth Narrator And, if it were possible, this news brought Mr and Mrs Prince closer together than ever.

No. 9 This Has To Be Love (v5)

Both (*singing happily*) This has to be love!
It really was love with our limbs intertwining
And now we have made, with our two seeds combining,
Prince (*placing his hand on her stomach*) Be here in a bit!
Aurora (*anxiously*) I'm sure it will fit.
Both That this really and truly,
Our passion's unruly,
This certainly has to be love!

The Prince and Aurora exit

Fourth Narrator Meanwhile ...

The Pigcutter appears with a piece of wood

... the Pigcutter to prove his undying love to Carabosse was working night and day —

Second Narrator — transforming the witch's cave into a veritable DIY palace with all manner of custom-built, individually designed stripped pine fitted units —

Pigcutter — the things we do for love —

Third Narrator But just occasionally the Pigcutter would pause in his labour of love to ask himself, truthfully, was Carabosse a woman who could lose her heart over custom-built stripped pine units?

Sixth Narrator Still, he wasn't fussed ... she could take it or leave it, couldn't she?

No. 10 Particular (Reprise)

Pigcutter I'm not particular, not that particular,
She does, she don't, we never could agree.
But for someone who's not specially particular
She's especially particular to me.

The Pigcutter goes

Sixth Narrator However, what he didn't know, indeed how could he know, was that Carabosse was now —

Narrators — a transformed woman ...

Underscore of expectation from the Narrators

The beautician's couch rises with Carabosse on it. Her face is swathed in bandages and her body completely covered. It all somewhat resembles a launch at a motor show

(*Variously, a muted musical rhubarb*) ... anticipation ... expectation ... mild elation ... trepidation ... celebration ...

De Vine enters and claps his hands for silence

A little sshh-ing

No. 11 Awaking Beauty

De Vine Dear friends, I invite to join here with me
For this, our awakening ceremony
(As previously witnessed on national TV).
Although it's symbolic, you have to agree,
It's also quite moving and touching to see.
I would just like to add, dearest colleagues of mine,
The undying thanks from one, Maurice De Vine.
It is now my pleasant duty
To commence awaking beauty

Narrators It is now our pleasant duty
To commence awaking beauty

During the next Carabosse is 'unwrapped' by the team

Awake! Awake, you beauty!
No sleeping your life away.
Mr Sun is up,
High time that you opened your eyes
Wake up, wake up, you beauty!
The start of a special new day
Time to rise and shine,
You're in for a gorgeous surprise!

During the next, on cue, De Vine kisses Carabosse lightly on the forehead. She wakes with a start and he helps her gently off the bed

You'll find your life now will seem a
Long continual moment of bliss,
Awaking this dreamer
To the sensation of the tenderest kiss

Under the next, a couple of the team wheel on a full length mirror

Arise! Arise, you beauty!
Rub sleep from your eyes, please do!
As the whole wide world awaits a brand new you,
Awake, awake, you beauty,
Say hallo —
To a beautiful view!

They now gently guide Carabosse to the mirror

Awake, awake, you beauty,
Say hallo —
To a beautiful you!

The song ends, they wait for her reaction. Carabosse studies herself long and hard

Carabosse (*at last, not disapprovingly*) Fuck me! (*Turning to De Vine*) What do you think?
De Vine Enchanting.
Carabosse Really?
De Vine My dear, you look absolutely stunning. Doesn't she?

General approval from the others

Carabosse Will men want to sleep with me, you reckon?
De Vine Oh, undoubtedly. Quite undoubtedly.
Carabosse Would you?
De Vine (*a trifle thrown*) Well — I'm — I'm perhaps not the man to ask, I — (*Turning to one of the others*) Geoff? Let's ask Geoff here. This is more his forte. What do you think, Geoff?
Geoff Me?
De Vine Yes.
Geoff Would I —— ?
De Vine Yes.

One of the other women is glaring at Geoff. He is a bit torn between her, De Vine and Carabosse

Geoff Er — Yes. Oh, yes.
Carabosse (*wiggling a hip at him*) Fancy a bit, do you?
Geoff Oh, yes.

Carabosse Well, you're not getting any, you pouff. (*She gives her old familiar laugh*) Ha-ha-ha-ha-ha-ha! Oh! (*She touches her face, puzzled*)

De Vine (*clapping his hands*) All right, everyone! That's it! Work to be done! Beauty never sleeps, not here!

The others disperse

Carabosse What's wrong with my face?

De Vine There's nothing wrong with it. It's perfect.

Carabosse Why can't I move it properly?

De Vine Well that's as a result of the treatment, I'm afraid. I — we gave it a few injections to encourage it to — relax.

Carabosse Feels like I've been out in a force nine gale.

De Vine Well, I'm sure you'll get used to it.

Carabosse As long as I can still get my mouth open. Ha-ha-ha-ha-ha-ha!

De Vine (*frowning*) Yes. I feel there may still be one or things to do in that department ...

Carabosse With my mouth?

De Vine Well ...

Carabosse Yes, I'll need to get used to these lips. Be a bit like kissing through an elf's arse otherwise, eh? Ha-ha-ha-ha-ha-ha!

De Vine There's no problem with your mouth, well not for a month or two anyway. It's rather more what comes out of it.

Carabosse Pardon?

De Vine The sound. It doesn't quite chime with your new image. I think, before you finally leave us, I'll arrange a session with our Miss Chasum. She works wonders with speech. I'll see if she's free. Wait there! Please wait there ... now I never did catch your first name ... it's —— ?

Carabosse Carabosse.

De Vine (*trying it*) Carabosse? Yes ...

Carabosse Though the nurses call me Cara for short.

De Vine Cara? Oh, yes that's so much prettier. If I were you, I'd stick to Cara. Won't be a second.

De Vine exits

Carabosse (*savouring her new name*) Cara? ... Cara ... (*She moves back to the mirror to admire herself. She becomes aware of her enhanced bust for the first time. Peering down the front of her gown*) Oh, hallo, you two! Can't even see my bloody feet, now, can I? All together now ... (*Improvising a little witch's jig and chanting*)

Wiggle, jiggle, primp, preen!
Who's the sweetest girl you've seen?

She encourages the Narrators to join in

Wiggle, jiggle, primp, preen!
Who's the fairest beauty queen?

Narrators Wiggle, jiggle, primp, preen!
Wiggle, jiggle, primp —

Miss Chasum, a rather prim speech therapist, enters briskly. She carries a clipboard

Carabosse and the Narrators stop abruptly

Miss Chasum Good morning! Good morning! Chasum. Natalie Chasum. Call me Nattie, everyone else does. Now then, Cara ... Cara isn't it? Pretty name. Cara, Mr De Vine has been telling me that you're having a little trouble with your speech, is that the case?

Carabosse Well, I —

Miss Chasum Now, tell me precisely, Cara, is it just with your diction — general pronunciation, particular vowels, or syllables? That sort of thing?

Carabosse No, I don't —

Miss Chasum In which case, there probably isn't any cause for alarm. Sometimes, we find you know that after a general anaesthetic your tongue can be the very last thing to wake up. A touch of STS. Snoozy Tongue Syndrome, I call it — (*She laughs*)

Carabosse No, I think —

Miss Chasum Or is it certain words you can't remember? Certain adjectives, verbs, adverbs, pronouns, conjunctions even?

Carabosse No, that certainly isn't —

Miss Chasum But you can see what I'm driving at. I'm simply trying to ascertain, Cara — I can call you Cara, can't I — please do call me Nattie, everyone else does — I'm simply trying to ascertain the precise nature of your speech problem. You see? Now tell me in your own words? What exactly's the problem? In your own words. Take your time.

Carabosse Well, from getting them in edgeways. Ha-ha-ha-ha-ha-ha! …

Miss Chasum (*frowning, consulting her clipboard*) Oh dear, yes. Mr De Vine mentioned the laugh. Yes ... would you mind doing it again for me, Cara? The laugh. Once more. Would you do it again for me, please?

Carabosse (*mirthlessly*) Ha-ha-ha! (*She pauses*) Well, I just can't laugh, can I? I need something to laugh at.

Miss Chasum Well, what sort of thing makes you laugh, Cara?

Carabosse I don't know. If you got up, fell flat on your stupid face and broke your nose, that might do it.

Miss Chasum Well, I certainly don't intend to do that.

Carabosse Pity, I could do with a good laugh. Ha-ha-ha-ha-ha-ha!

Miss Chasum Cara, I have to say, that's not very melodic, is it, now? A lovely woman like you, that's such an ugly sound coming from that pretty mouth. The laugh of a beautiful woman, Cara, should be like a cool clear waterfall in springtime. Yours is more like a — blocked winter drain. Let's try a few exercises, shall we? Now, after me: — (*She sings*)

No.12 Laughing Song

Ha! Ha! Ha! Ha-ha! Ha! Ha!
Carabosse (*copying her, reluctantly at first*)
Ha! Ha! Ha! Ha-ha! Ha! Ha!

Miss Chasum (*speaking*) Jolly good, dear! (*She sings*)

Hee! Hee! Hee! Hee-hee! Hee! Hee!
Carabosse Hee! Hee! Hee! Hee-hee! Hee! Hee!

Miss Chasum (*speaking*) Well done! (*She sings*)

Ho! Ho! Ho! Ho-ho! Ho! Ho!
Carabosse Ho! Ho! Ho! Ho-ho! Ho! Ho!

Miss Chasum (*speaking*) Splendid, Cara! (*She sings*)

Woo-hoo-hoo! Hoo-hoo! Woo-hoo!
Carabosse Woo-hoo-hoo! Hoo-hoo! Woo-hoo!

Miss Chasum (*speaking*) And once again! (*She sings*)

Ha! ha! ha! ha-ha! ha!
Carabosse (*beginning to enjoy it*)
Ha! Ha! Ha! Ha-ha! Ha!
Miss Chasum Hee! Hee! Hee! Hee-hee! Hee!
Carabosse Hee! Hee! Hee! Hee-hee! Hee!
Miss Chasum Ho! Ho! Ho! Ho-ho! Ho!

Carabosse Ho! Ho! Ho! Ho-ho! Ho!
Miss Chasum Woo-hoo-hoo! Hoo-hoo! Hoo-hoo!
Carabosse Hoo! Hoo! Hoo! Hoo-hoo! Hoo!

Miss Chasum Ha! Ha! Ha-ha! Ha! Ha!
Carabosse Hee! Hee-hee! Hee! Hee!
Miss Chasum Ho! Ho! Ho! Ho-ho! Ho!
Carabosse Hoo! Hoo! Hoo-hoo!
Miss Chasum Ha! Ha! Ha! Ha-ha! Ha!
Carabosse Hee! Hee! Hee! Hee-hee! Hee!
Miss Chasum Ho! Ho! Ho! Ho-ho! Ho!
Carabosse Woo! Hoo! Hoo!

Miss Chasum (*speaking*) Super! Let's try our vowels now, shall we? (*She sings*)

I say, no way can they
Come out to play today.
Carabosse I say, no way can they
Come out to play today.
Miss Chasum Can thee and me agree
To have green peas for tea?
Carabosse Can thee and me agree
To have green peas for tea?
Miss Chasum I think you'll find that I
Like spicy ice rice pie!
Carabosse I think you'll find that I
Like spicy ice rice pie!
Miss Chasum Usually you should choose
Two true confusing views
Carabosse Usually you should choose
Two true confusing views

Miss Chasum (*speaking*) Oh, isn't this fun? (*She sings*)

Ha! Ha! Ha! Ha-ha! Ha!
Carabosse Ha! Ha! Ha! Ha-ha! Ha!
Miss Chasum Hee! Hee! Hee! Hee-hee! Hee!
Carabosse Hee! Hee! Hee! Hee-hee! Hee!
Miss Chasum Ho! Ho! Ho! Ho-ho! Ho!
Carabosse Ho! Ho! Ho! Ho-ho! Ho!

Miss Chasum (*speaking*) And — together! (*She sings*)

Miss Chasum Woo-hoo-hoo! Hoo-hoo! Woo!
Carabosse Woo-hoo-hoo! Hoo-hoo-hoo-hoo!
Miss Chasum Ha! Ha! Ha! Ha-ha! Ha! Ha!
Carabosse Ha! Ha-ha!
Miss Chasum Hee! Hee! Hee! Hee-hee!
Carabosse Hee! Hee! Hee-hee-hee-hee!
Miss Chasum Ho! Ho! Ho! Ho-ho! Ho!
Carabosse Ho-ho-ho! Ho! Ho! Ho!
Miss Chasum Woo-hoo-hoo! Hoo-hoo! Hoo!
Carabosse Ha! Ha! Ha! Ha! Ha! Ha! Ha! Ha!

The others join in

All Hee-hee-hee! Hee-hee! Hee!
Ha-ha-ha-ha-ha-ha-ha-ha-ha-ha-ha-ha-ha!

They finish the song quite elated

Miss Chasum You know, I never cease to enjoy that! Keep working on that, won't you. Practice makes perfect, remember. Oh, I'm very late. Must dash. Bye. (*She hurries to the door. She trips slightly*) Whoops!
Carabosse (*reverting to her original laugh*) Ha-ha-ha-ha-ha-ha!
Miss Chasum (*a trifle dismayed*) Yes, well do work on it, won't you, dear?

Miss Chasum goes out

Carabosse lies back. As she starts to practice her new laugh the bed descends

Carabosse (*as she goes*) Ha! ha! ha! ha-ha! ha! ha!
Hee! hee! hee! hee-hee! hee! hee!

The Lights crossfade to the next scene

Scene 2

The hospital waiting-room

The Prince appears, pacing anxiously

First Narrator In the meantime, unknown to Carabosse, or Cara as we must now call her, in a hospital quite nearby, Mr Prince was anxiously awaiting a happy event.

No. 13 Multiple Birth Refrain

Nurses (*off*) Another deep breath, Mama!
And *push*!
Just one final shove, *comme ça*!
Aurora (*off, in labour*) Aa-aahhh!
Nurses (*off*) Your baby is nearly due
Prince (*empathizing, wincing*) Ooo-ooh!
Nurses (*off*) That's it!
And *push*! And *push*!
Aurora (*off*) Aa-aa-aa-ah!
Prince (*wincing*) Oo-oo-oo-oo!
Nurses (*off*) And one more *push*!!!!
Aurora (*off, a final big shove*) Aa-ah!
Prince (*with her*) Oo-oo-oo-ooh!
Nurses (*off, triumphantly, with her*) Yeeeesssss!!
1st Baby (*off*) Wah! Wah! Wah! Wah!
Nurses (*off*) It's a little boy!
Bravo!
Prince (*quietly, punching the air, delighted*) Yes!

Slight pause

Nurses (*off*) She's starting again there's two
And push!
Another is coming through
Aurora (*off, in labour*) Ooh-ooh!
Nurses (*off*) The head is emerging now
Prince (*empathizing, wincing*) Oh, wow!
Nurses (*off*) That's it! And *push*! And *push*!
Aurora (*off*) Aa-aa-aa-aa!
Prince (*wincing*) Oo-oo-oo-oo!
Nurses (*off*) And one more *push*!!!!
Aurora (*off, a final big shove*) Aa-aa!
Prince (*with her*) Oo-oo-oo-oo!
Nurses (*off, triumphantly, with her*) Yeeeesssss!!
2nd Baby (*off*) Wah! Wah! Wah! Wah! Wah!
Nurses (*off*) It's another little boy!
Hooray!
Prince (*rather less overjoyed than before*) Jolly good ...

Slight pause

Nurses (*off*) She's going for number three

Aurora (*off, in labour*) No more!
Nurses (*off*) Triplets! Just wait and see!
Aurora (*off, in labour*) Eeh-eehh!
Nurses (*off*) And who's been a clever girl?
Prince (*empathizing, wincing*) Good grief!
Nurses (*off*) Once more!
Aurora (*off, in labour*) Yes!
Nurses (*off*) Push!
Aurora (*off, in labour*) Aahh!
Nurses (*off*) Yes!
3rd Baby Wah!
Nurses (*off*) Yes!
3rd Baby Wah! Wah!
Nurses (*off*) It's another little boy!
All Oh yes!

Pause while the Prince recovers

Prince Heavens! I don't ever want to go through that again. I'm absolutely exhausted.

A Midwife pops in briefly, rather wearily

Midwife Mr Prince?
Prince Yes?
Midwife I am happy to tell you that your wife has —
Prince Yes. Three. I was counting.
Midwife — little boys —
Prince Yes, I heard. Push by shove.
Midwife Congratulations!
Prince May I possibly — see —
Midwife The babies? Well, perhaps a quick look. They're all perfectly fit and healthy, you don't need to worry. (*Making to leave*) Congratulations again. They're just through here if you want a quick peep.

The Midwife goes

Prince (*calling after her, vainly*) No, I rather meant, see my ... wife. See babies, any old time. Seen one baby you've seen them all ...
First Narrator And the prince decided to creep in to see his beloved wife.

Aurora comes on, asleep on a hospital bed

And the moment he caught sight of Aurora, his heart filled with love for her. In fact, he was reminded of the moment he had very first caught sight of her.

The Prince moves to her bedside. He bends to kiss her on the lips

Prince (*singing softly*) This has to be …
Aurora (*the moment she is touched, loudly*) Aaaaaaaaaaaaaahhhhhhh!!!

The Prince jumps back, alarmed. Aurora opens her eyes and sits up staring wildly, not seeing him

(*In horror*) No more! No more! Please, no more!

Her nightmare over, she drops back on to the pillow and closes her eyes again

Prince (*rather nervously*) I'll — er ... I'll just pop through here and visit the little chaps.

The Prince goes out as Aurora's bed goes off

The Lights crossfade to the next scene

Scene 3

The City streets

Second Narrator And at that precise moment, Cara left the clinic and stepped out into the streets in search of her Prince. A new woman meeting a new world.

During the following, Carabosse enters, now dressed in elegant clothes and looking good. Incongruously she still carries her now much depleted bag of gold

No.14 Busy in the City (Refrain)

Narrators It's busy, busy, busy in the city.
Busy city, busy city, busy city,
Beep-beep! Vroom-vroom! Crash-bang! Shout-shout!
Yeehaw, yeehaw! Paarrpp-paarrrp! Look out!

Carabosse stares around her for a moment

It's hustle, bustle-bustle in the city,
Busy city, busy city, busy city.

As she steps forward into the road, various male voices greet her from on high

Men (*variously, from a distant building site*)
Wey-hey! Get that! Dar-ling! Yoo hoo!
Hal-lo! Great tits! Coo-eee!
Carabosse (*angrily*) Eff-you!

Second Narrator Cara was going to have to get used to the stares and unwarranted attention.

As she moves on the Narrators male and female, pass her staring

Carabosse becomes rather self-conscious

Narrators It's muscle tussle-tussle in the city,
Women (*variously*) Simply lovely, oh, she's gorgeous, very pretty,
Men (*variously*) You first, my dear, — watch out, don't fall!
Do you — need help — with that — at all?

Carabosse (*speaking*) Piss off!

Narrators It's busy, busy, busy in the city.
Busy city, busy city, busy city,
Beep-beep! Vroom-vroom! Crash-bang! Shout-shout!
Yeehaw, yeehaw! Paarrpp-paarrrp! Look out!

Carabosse, eventually panicked by all the attention, ducks into a side-street

The passers-by go

Carabosse (*breathlessly*) Oh, God! (*She stands breathing deeply, recovering*)

Second Narrator Cara eventually took refuge in a side street. Not only was she finding this new image very hard to cope with, she was also finding it quite difficult to breathe, owing to the constrictive nature of her underclothing. That, coupled with a pair of shoes that were practically impossible even to cross the street in, life was becoming a challenge. Thankfully, her once weighty bag of gold was now considerably lighter.

Third Narrator And as she stood in a side-street in the doorway of an ironmongers, who should emerge from the shop but —

First Narrator (*as a shop bell*) Jingle — jingle — jingle ...

The Pigcutter comes out, clutching a brown paper bag

He nearly collides with Carabosse, gives her a quick apologetic glance but fails to recognize her

Pigcutter Beg your pardon, madam. Excuse me. (*He starts to move on*)

Carabosse Pig!

Pigcutter Sorry?

Carabosse Pig!

Pigcutter Sorry. I said I'm sorry. No need to get like that.

Carabosse Pig, it's me. Carabosse! Cara.

Pigcutter I'm sorry, there's been some —

Carabosse It is! It's me, Pig!

Pigcutter I think you must be mistaking me for another pig of the same name — we do tend to look a bit alike. I mean, not to other pigs, of course. We can always tell the difference — it's the same with cows. Now, to me or you, one cow looks very much the same as another cow. Whereas to another cow —

Carabosse (*angrily*) Will you shut up, you stupid bloody pig. Or I'll slit your nasty little throat and slice you into smoked bacon!

Silence. He stares at her

Pigcutter (*in stunned amazement*) Mistress? Mistress, it's you! It's really you.

Carabosse I told you. What are you doing in the City, pig? Who gave you permission to be here?

Pigcutter I just slipped out to buy some more woodscrews, that's all. Listen, what have you — what have they — ? What's happened to you?

Carabosse I've — had a makeover, haven't I? You like it?

Pigcutter Well. You're different, I'll say that. I mean, not inside you're not. You're the same inside, talking to you ...

Carabosse (*impatiently*) So what do you think of the outside? Do you like it?

Pigcutter I could probably get used to it. In time.
Carabosse Do you think I'm sexy? Do you find me sexy?
Pigcutter Well, depends what you mean by sexy.
Carabosse (*pointing to her breasts*) What about these?
Pigcutter Oh, yes they're — they're pretty big.
Carabosse Oh, you're no use. No point in asking a pig, is there? My beloved's all that matters. Do you think he'll find me sexy? My prince?
Pigcutter Oh, him. Possibly. He'll probably fall for all that. He's the sort of bloke who'd go for, you know — additional extras.
Carabosse So long as he's — attracted to me. So long as he finds me — you know ...
Pigcutter Beddable.
Carabosse Don't be coarse! Go on, pig, piss off home!
Pigcutter Where are you going, now?
Carabosse To start looking for him. My prince.

Intro underscore starts under the following

Pigcutter Listen, before you do ... You don't think there'd be any chance of — lifting the curse off me, would you? Only I'm doing a spot of improvement — just the occasional shelf, cupboard, kitchen cabinet, nothing for you to worry about — only I'm finding it quite tricky to, you know, to handle the tools, like ...
Carabosse Listen, pig, prick up those porky little ears for a minute ... (*She sings*)

No. 15 Only Then

If you think I've made this transformation,
Without a minute's pause or hesitation
And taken leave of all my common sense,
For nothing
I've undergone the pain, the degradation,
The ridicule, the sheer humiliation,
For nothing.
Then I'd like you, pig, to know,
By all the darkest powers that lie below
I hereby swear I'll never sleep again
Till I've achieved this basic when and then ...

When I introduce my prince,
To this perfect me.
When I've wooed and won his heart,

When so e'er that be
When I see his princess bride,
Shedding bitter tears,
When I steal her love away —
Pigcutter This could take you years.
Carabosse When I bring him home at last,
When my heart does break
Bursting full of love for him —
Pigcutter How long will that take?
Carabosse When I shed salt tears of joy,
Gain my powers again —

Pigcutter Then perhaps you'll set me free?
Carabosse Then only then!

(*Speaking*) Now go home and don't bother me any more!

Carabosse leaves

The Pigcutter stares after her

Pigcutter (*dismayed*) That'll take her ages! She's got to find him first. (*Calling after her*) I should try the phone book! Under P for Prince Charming!

He leaves in a different direction

As he does so, the Lights change to the next scene

Scene 4

Aurora and the Prince's bedroom in their tiny flat at 29 Brown Brick Road

It is dark except for light leaking in from the street

Both are lying in their narrow bed. In the corner of the room, a triple crib in which, momentarily, sleep three small babies

Third Narrator At number 29 Brown Brick Road in their tiny flat, Mr and Mrs Prince were trying to snatch an hour or two of sleep in their tiny single bed in their minuscule bedroom. The room was made to feel even smaller now, since the recent arrival of their bonny babies, Arthur, Boris and Conrad, all named after relatives of Mr Prince. Mrs Prince had, of course, observed that their boys' names had been chosen alphabetically. Given the size of Mr Prince's family, it was with some concern that Aurora vaguely recalled that the alphabet still had twenty-three remaining letters.

Fourth Narrator At present, neither of them could enjoy a single moment of sleep. Both were wide awake, though keeping as still as possible, considerately trying not to wake their partner whom they assumed was asleep.

Fifth Narrator Both were in fact waiting for the sound of the cries of either Arthur or Boris or Conrad waking up to demand food which they did day and night, every hour on the hour. Unfortunately, their hours never started at the same moment.

A Baby Fugue. Each child joining the other in a wordless and increasingly complex counterpoint, growing louder, till all six Narrators' voices are eventually joined. At the start though it is baby Conrad who starts up. Voiced by Fourth Narrator, he jiggles restlessly in the cot

Fourth Narrator (*as Baby Conrad*) Wa-wa-wa-wa-wah-wa-wa-wah-wah-wah-wah. (*Etc.*)

The parents both talk over this, also quietly at first but getting progressively louder

Prince Oh, God!
Aurora Oh, no!
Prince Here we go again.

They listen for a second

Which one's that? Boris?
Aurora No, that's Conrad, again.
Prince They all sound the same to me. You want me to fetch him over, darling? So you can top him up?
Aurora (*wearily*) Oh, yes, you might as well, darling ...

The Prince gets out of bed and gropes his way to the crib. Baby Conrad continues under

Prince I can't see a thing ... (*Stubbing his toe*) Ow! Need a bit of light.
Aurora Well don't switch the light on, darling! Or they'll all wake up!

Prince (*reaching the crib*) OK! OK! I've found him. Hang on, darling! Come on! Here we go, you greedy little devil.

The Prince lifts a baby from the crib. The Second Narrator as Baby Boris now joins in with Baby Conrad

Fifth Narrator (*as Boris, with Conrad*) Goo-goo-goo-goo-googy-goo-goo-goo … (*Etc.*)
Prince Damn! I've picked up the wrong one, darling.
Aurora (*slightly crossly*) That's Boris! Now you've woken Boris up, darling!
Prince (*indignantly, making his way back to the bed with Boris*) Well, it's pitch dark, darling! How am I supposed to tell Boris from Conrad? They all look the same to me, anyway.
Aurora Will you please stop shouting, darling!

Baby Arthur joins in

Sixth Narrator (*as Arthur, joining with the others*) Ma-ma-ma-ma-ma-ma-ma-ma-ma … (*Etc.*)
Aurora Oh no, now there's Arthur!
Prince (*handing her the baby*) Here!
Aurora This is Boris.
Prince I know it's Boris.
Aurora (*putting the baby to her breast*) Well, it wasn't Boris who woke up!
Prince Well he's awake now.
Aurora (*removing the baby again*) He's not even hungry, darling. Take him back and bring me Conrad.
Prince (*wearily*) OK, OK, OK. Sorry darling.

He takes Boris from her and goes cautiously back to the crib. The three babies continue

(*As he does so*) You want me to — ow —— ?
Aurora Careful, don't drop him, darling!
Prince (*reaching the crib*) — you want me to bring Arthur over, darling?
Aurora No. Just bring Conrad, darling. Conrad's the one that's hungry. Arthur's isn't hungry.
Prince (*replacing Boris in the crib*) How on earth can you tell?

The Prince removes another baby and makes his way back to her. During the next, the baby underscore gradually increases in volume

Aurora I'm their mother, darling, I can tell when my baby's hungry.

Prince Come on you hungry little so and so! (*Returning and handing her the baby*) There you are, darling.

Aurora Thank you, darling. (*She puts the baby to her breast and snatches it away again*) This is Arthur, darling. I want Conrad. Why did you bring me Arthur when I specifically asked for Conrad? First you bring me Boris and then you bring me Arthur. (*Bouncing up and down in the bed crossly*) Conrad! Conrad! Conrad!

Prince (*angrily*) All right! All right! All right, darling! It's pitch dark, the room's full of identical babies, all yelling their heads off. Now come on be fair! Don't you start yelling at me, as well!

A brief silence. It is now quieter again

And you've been told, if you bounce up and down like that, darling, you'll curdle.

Aurora (*chastened, meekly*) I'm sorry, darling. Do you want to switch the light on, would that help?

Prince (*sulkily*) Yes. That's what I wanted to do in the first place, darling.

Aurora What's it matter? We're all awake now, anyway.

He switches on the light. The Baby fugue starts up again in full flow with all six Narrators in full voice

Prince (*startled, over the din*) What the —— ?

Aurora (*shouting*) Oh, no — we've woken up the neighbours' babies again! We'll never get any sleep, now ...

As the fugue continues, the two continue to communicate only in inaudible dumb show.

Aurora retains baby Arthur, who decides that after all, perhaps he did fancy a snack. The Prince meantime has gone and fetched Baby Conrad and brings him over to Aurora who clamps him to her other breast. The Prince then returns to the crib and brings over Baby Boris who he proffers to Aurora who indicates she has now run out of food sources. The Prince sits on the bed and jiggles Baby Boris

The fugue continues. As the bed goes, it continues and then ends abruptly

Scene 5

The City streets

Carabosse enters, tired and rather less groomed than before. She pauses for breath in the quiet street.

The Narrators give a low skyline hum of distant traffic

Narrators Brrrmm-brrrmmm-brrrmmm-brrrrmmm.

Third Narrator (*over this*) After a week or two, Cara had all but given up ever finding her prince. But although her feet were sore and aching almost as badly as her heart, she refused to abandon the search for the man she loved and she believed, if they met again, would now truly fall in love with her.

Second Narrator In the first few days she stayed at a large expensive hotel in the city centre, in keeping with her new glamorous image but, as the days passed, and she saw her already depleted supply of gold rapidly running out, she moved to smaller more modestly priced hotels.

First Narrator Eventually, she was forced to move way out into an unfashionable suburb, where she felt sure her prince would never deign to live. Still, needs must ...

Fourth Narrator She was now staying in a cheap self-catering hotel situated on the edge of the main railway line where, from her filthy fifth floor window, she also had a perfect view of the city inner ring road. Still, Cara was used to discomfort and the room reminded her nostalgically somewhat of home.

Fifth Narrator But now she was hungry and had left her hotel in search of food, preferably the cheaper the better.

Sixth Narrator Suddenly, she saw on a street corner one of the dingiest cut-price supermarkets she had ever seen in her life ...

Carabosse moves to the doorway and enters

Narrators (*shop bell*) Brrriiiinnnggg!

The supermarket is marked by a single cash till, at which sits a bored Girl, reading a magazine

The Narrators now start up with the supermarket muzak we heard earlier. Carabosse steps in cautiously. She moves a few paces and hesitates

Carabosse Excuse me. I wonder if you could tell me where I can find —

Girl (*bored, without looking up*) Sorry, busy. Someone round the back can help you.

Carabosse glares at her and makes one of her old spell gestures in frustration. As she moves away, the Girl watches her slyly from over her magazine. Carabosse wanders further into the shop. She still can't see what she wants

Carabosse (*scanning the shelves*) Mushrooms … mushrooms … it's all bloody mushrooms. God what I wouldn't give for a decent toadstool! (*Frustratedly*) Oh, this is ridiculous. (*Calling*) Hallo! Someone? Anybody here?

The Prince stumbles in from a storeroom wearing his shop overall. He has evidently been asleep

Carabosse gapes at him in amazement. He fails to recognize her

Prince Hi, somebody call — I — (*Seeing Carabosse*) Oh. Hallo, there. Can I help?

The supermarket muzak switches to a schmaltzy version of This Has to Be Love!

Carabosse (*lost for words*) I — er — I — er —

Prince Sorry. I was just in the stockroom there grabbing a quick forty — grabbing forty — tins of — something or other. What can I do for you?

Carabosse You're working here?

Prince Yes.

Carabosse I see.

Prince Is there — something I can help you with?

Carabosse (*staring at him*) I'm sure you can ...

The narration adopts a rather romantic fiction tone

First Narrator Cara's heart was beating rapidly. She was aware of his eyes studying her new breasts. She tried desperately to control her breathing, telling herself, whatever happened, to behave normally. Suddenly, gloriously, wonderfully, there he was standing right before her. What was she to do? All her previous carefully laid plans, her artful stratagems, lay in ruins. She couldn't lose him again now. She couldn't ... ?

Prince (*tearing his gaze away from her bust*) Well, if you'll excuse me, I must just get back to — er — counting things ... (*He starts to back away*)

First Narrator It was now or never.

Carabosse Actually I'm desperate to find some green peas.

Prince (*puzzled*) Sorry?

Carabosse Green peas. For my tea.

Prince Oh, green peas.

Carabosse Do you keep green peas?

Prince Oh, yes, tinned or frozen?

Carabosse Oh tinned.

Prince Right. Just follow me.

He takes her round a couple of corners

Carabosse (*following him*) I don't have a freezer, you see. So I'm not able to freeze peas.

Prince Oh, that's a bit tiresome for you.

They arrive at a pyramid of cans of peas

There you go. I just arranged them this morning. Take your pick!

Carabosse How lovely. (*She bends, seductively, to take a can from the base of the pile*) Thank you.

Prince Oh, I wouldn't take one from there! You'll have the whole lot down. I've done that a few times, myself. Here, allow me.

He bends to push back the tin she has dislodged. Carabosse whimpers at this sight

(*Handing her a fresh can from the top*) There, you go.

Carabosse (*standing close to him*) Thank you.

Prince Want anything else?

Carabosse Oh, yes. Yes, lots more.

Prince Peas?

Carabosse Please.

Prince Well, I'll tell you what, if you're into peas in a big way, which you obviously are, then may I suggest you'd do better to buy them in bulk. Work out a lot cheaper. Can I interest you in a case, at all?

First Narrator She could feel his warm breath on her cheek. She heard a voice, she recognized as her own, whispering —

Carabosse (*whispering*) Oh, yes, yes, yes.
Prince Righty-ho. Hang on there. Just one second.

The Prince goes off, briefly

Carabosse does a twirl

First Narrator She felt giddy with excitement. As though her feet were about to dance of their own accord right there in the supermarket aisle ...

Carabosse starts to dance

The Prince returns with a large cardboard carton, filled with cans of peas

Carabosse stops dancing

Prince Here we are. Now, this is a brand new case. It hasn't even been opened. One hundred and forty-four tins. Not too many, is it?
Carabosse No.
Prince Tell you what, it's a bit of a weight — would you like me to carry it for you? Just as far as your ——
Carabosse Thank you!
First Narrator She saw through the texture of his shirt, the outline of the firm strong muscles of his biceps ...
Prince Follow me then!
Carabosse Oh, yes. (*Laughing her new laugh*) Ha! Ha! Ha! Ha-ha! Ha! Ha!

The Prince leads Carabosse out of the shop passing the Girl who is still reading her magazine

Prince (*as they pass*) Back in a tick, Gretel.

The Prince and Carabosse go out

Girl Is she going to be paying for — ? (*Calling after them*) I say, excuse me!

After a second she shrugs and returns to her magazine. The cash till and the display go

The Lights crossfade to a brief inset scene: the mouth of the cave

The Pigcutter enters, weary and depressed, taking a break from his labours, holding the turned leg of a coffee table. He sniffs the fresh air

Birdsong from the Narrators

Pigcutter (*looking hopefully*) Cara? (*He listens*) Cara? That you? (*Shaking his head*) No. (*Gloomily studying the table leg*) I'm beginning to lose heart a bit with all this, I don't mind saying.

He goes back in again, rather sadly

As he does so the Lights fade on him and the scene changes

Scene 6

The living area of Carabosse's small, dingy self-catering hotel room

The bedroom is off through another door. There is, at least, a battered sofa and armchair

Carabosse and the Prince, still carrying the case of tinned peas, enter. She turns on the light

Carabosse Here we are. Home at last.
Prince (*looking round*) Oh — interesting room. Where do you want these?
Carabosse Oh, just down there for now. This is so kind of you.

The Prince puts down the case, obviously glad to do so

Prince That's better. No, as I say, when I said I'd carry it for you I only sort of meant as far as your car.
Carabosse I don't have a car.
Prince As we subsequently discovered. Still. Jolly nice walk.
Carabosse Please do sit down a moment. May I offer you something to drink?
Prince (*sitting on the sofa*) Oh, thanks. Get my breath back. Lot of stairs in this place, aren't there?
Carabosse Glass of beer? Whisky? Vodka?
Prince God! Bit early for all that, isn't it? A glass of water would hit the spot.

Carabosse (*slightly dismayed*) Glass of water?
Prince Just the ticket.

Carabosse goes off

Interesting sort of hotel, this. Do you stay here a lot?
Carabosse (*off*) Oh yes. I'm wildly fond of it. (*Her new laugh*) Ha! Ha! Ha! Ha-ha! Ha! Ha!
Prince Yes, I noticed it does seem to cater for a lot of single women. Very friendly bunch, aren't they?
Carabosse (*off*) Oh, yes.

Carabosse returns with a glass of water

Prince All smiling. Yes, of course a woman like you on her own, you must —

The Narrators interrupt him with the sound of a loud train approaching and passing the window. Everything vibrates in the room including Carabosse's water glass

All (*as the train passes*) Ruckerty-tung — ruckerty-tung — ruckerty-tung … (*Etc.*)

The train recedes

Prince (*startled*) What in the name of heaven earth was that?
Carabosse Oh, just the railway. Here. (*She gives him the glass*)
Prince Sounds as if it was coming through here. (*Taking the glass*) Thanks. Do they pass through this room often? (*He laughs*)
Carabosse Ha! Ha! Ha! Ha-ha! Ha! Ha! Oh, no. Once every twenty minutes, if that.
Prince Heavens. I thought our place was noisy enough.
Carabosse Do you have a lovely home? (*She sits by him*) I bet you have a gorgeous home, don't you?
Prince Well, it has its moments. I have a gorgeous wife, which makes up for the décor. (*He laughs, then drains the glass in one*)

Carabosse growls and hisses slightly at the mention of Aurora

(*Finishing the water*) Thanks. Terrific water. Sorry? Did you say something?
Carabosse (*deciding on action, taking the empty glass from him*) Please. If you can stay just one second longer —

She switches on some music which the Narrators provide. A smoochy version of This Has to Be Love!

Relax! I need to show you something I think you'll enjoy.

Prince What's that?

Carabosse (*moving to the door*) A surprise. (*In the doorway*) Wait there.

She fiddles with the light switches making the room first brighter and then darker

That's better. Please. Won't be a tick. Relax.

Carabosse goes out

Prince (*a bit puzzled by all this*) I can't stay too long. I have to get back to work. Or they'll dock my pay. Then I'll be in trouble with my wife. *(Laughing)* She probably won't let me in the front door.

No reply from the other room

(*Swinging his legs up on to the sofa*) God, I'm tired — didn't get a lot of shut-eye last night ... (*He yawns*) … still that's par for the ... par for the ... (*Yawning again*) … didn't get a lot of sheep ... did I say sheep? ... I meant sheep ... sheep... sheep... (*He falls asleep*)

Carabosse, in a second, returns, she wears a negligé over some skimpy night attire

She sees him and smiles. On impulse, she bends over the back of the sofa to kiss him. As she is about to do so, another train thunders past

Narrators (*a train passing*) Ruckerty-tung — ruckerty-tung — ruckerty-tung … (*Etc.*)

Carabosse draws back, startled. Simultaneously, the Prince awakes with a start and rolls off the sofa on to the floor

Prince (*jumping to his feet, blearily*) My God! Was I asleep? How long have I been asleep? I must get back. Sorry. Cheerio! Otherwise, my wife will have a fit!

The Prince rushes out, not giving Carabosse a glance

Carabosse (*grinding her teeth with frustration*) That's not quite what I had in mind for her. But close enough! Close enough!

As she turns to go back into her bedroom, another train passes

Narrators Ruckerty-tung — ruckerty-tung — ruckerty —
Carabosse (*savagely to them*) Oh, just shut up!

They do

She goes out

The Lights fade and the scene changes

Scene 7

Aurora and the Prince's small sitting-room in their tiny flat at 29 Brown Brick Road

There is a sofa, an armchair and a small low table. In one corner is the crib with the triplets, all asleep

Second Narrator Back at 29 Brown Brick Road, in the living-room of their tiny flat, tension between Mr and Mrs Prince was beginning to grow.

The Prince comes on, angrily from the bedroom, pulling on his jacket. An anxious Aurora follows, still in her dressing-gown

Prince (*angrily*) ... I'm not discussing this now, darling, I have to go to work ...
Aurora (*distressed*) But we have to talk about it. All I'm saying is, we need to sit down and discuss this ——
Prince NOT NOW! I've said not now. I'm very late. If I'm any later I'll get the sack and then we'll have no money at all, will we? See you tonight! We'll talk about it then.
Aurora (*calling after him despairingly*) You keep saying that, we never do. And don't slam the front ——
Narrators Slaaammm!!!!
Aurora — or you'll wake the ——

In the crib, Arthur, Basil and Conrad wake up

Fourth Narrator (*as Conrad*) Wah-wah-wah-wah-wah-wah-wah-wah-wah-wah-wah. (*Etc.*)

Fifth Narrator (*as Boris, with Conrad*) Goo-goo-goo-goo-goo-goo-goo-goo. (*Etc.*)

Sixth Narrator (*as Arthur, joining in*) Lo-lo-lo-lo-lo-lo-lo-lo-lo-lo-lo. (*Etc.*)

Aurora Oh, no! All right, darlings. (*On the verge of tears*) It's only Daddy — slamming the — as he does every single morning, lately — Mummy's here now ... Mummy's here ...

She hums the intro, the babies quieten. As she sings, they join in with her and then, one by one, fall asleep

No. 16 Aurora's Lullaby

Hush-hush, hush-hush, my dear little boys,
Sleep now, go to sleep, Mummy's here.
Sleep well, sweet dreams — let's hear no more noise,
She's here, very close, never fear.
You're comfort'bly cosily snug in bed,
It's time you were snoozing, you sweet sleepy head.
Dee-doo, dee-doo — dee-dee-dee-dee-dee
Dee-dee-dee-dee-dee-dee good night.

Fourth Narrator (*as Conrad*) } Wah-wah-wah-wah-wah-wah-wah-wah-wah.
Aurora (*with him*) } Dee-dee-dee-dee-dee-dee-dee-dee-dee.
Fifth Narrator (*as Boris*) } Goo-goo-goo-goo-goo-goo-goo.
Aurora (*with him*) } Dee-dee-dee-dee-dee-dee-dee.
Sixth Narrator (*as Arthur*) } Lo-lo-lo-lo-.
Aurora (*with him*) } Dee-dee-dee-dee.
Aurora Dee-doo, dee-doo — dee-dee-dee-dee-dee
Dee-dee-dee-dee-dee-dee dee night

As the lullaby ends, there is a moment's blissful silence

Narrators (*as the front doorbell*) Brrriiinnnggg!

Aurora Oh, no, no, no, no, no, please! Don't wake up, again! Please don't wake up. Who can that be?

She goes to the front door. She returns with Carabosse now transformed into her new chic businesswoman image, smart suit, briefcase etc. She has evidently pushed past the flustered Aurora

Carabosse So sorry to bother you. I promise, I won't take more than a moment of your time.

Aurora (*in an undertone*) Well, if you could just be terribly quiet. My children ... I've only just this minute got them to sleep, you see ...

Carabosse Oh, is this them? May I? (*Looking into the crib*) Oh, aren't they absolutely *scrumptious*? (*Smacking her lips*) Almost good enough to eat.

Aurora Yes ... if you could please be very quiet.

Carabosse (*adopting a quieter tone*) Yes, as I say, I'm from the W.A.M.B. The Woman's Apple Marketing Board and we're conducting a survey in this area —

Aurora (*protesting, ineffectually*) Well, I don't think we're really that interested —

Carabosse (*ploughing on, threatening to get louder*) ... a survey in this area, to test consumers' reaction to a new type of apple which we're considering marketing.

Uninvited, Carabosse sits on the sofa and puts her briefcase on the coffee table

May I — ? (*Opening her case*) Now, all that's required of you is that I leave you this delicious rosy red apple and ask you to taste it and judge it for flavour ...

Aurora Oh, I see. Is that all it is? Well, I'm very fond of apples as a matter of fact ...

Carabosse Yes, I thought you might be. There, isn't she a beauty? (*She puts a red apple on the table*)

Aurora Oh, yes, it does look nice. May I — ?

Carabosse Of course. It's all for you.

Aurora Thank you. Lovely, a free apple.

Carabosse Would you care to taste it now?

Aurora Well, I think if you don't mind, I'll wait for my husband ... we usually do things together, you see.

Carabosse Oh, dear me, no! It's not for your husband!

Aurora Why not?

Carabosse We're the *W*.A.M.B. The *Woman's* Apple Marketing Board. We don't want greedy men involved, do we?

Aurora No?

Carabosse Not at this delicate stage.

Aurora I see. Well ...

She plays nervously with the apple for a moment, as if undecided. Carabosse watches her

Carabosse I must tell you, there is a further inducement to take part in our survey, if you're interested. Should you agree to help us, there's also a *huge* cash sum to be won. Depending on whether you're the lucky woman to be drawn out of our hat.

Aurora Oh, I see. May I ask how much?

Carabosse Oh, a simply enormous sum. *Vast*.

Aurora (*still deliberating*) Yes, well I'm — tempted. I'm really very tempted. We could really do with the money, you see. I never believed that money was all that important before, you know. Probably because when I was young we always seemed to have masses and masses. But now we've got — almost nothing — well, you can see — and with the children growing — and my huband's not earning that much — and — er ... it's all desperately worrying, you see. (*Starting to cry*) I don't honestly know which way to turn. What to do for the best, really ...

Carabosse (*seemingly concerned*) Oh, poor you. Poor, poor you! Well, testing the apple might help. It could solve everything.

Aurora Yes ...

Carabosse The end of all your problems.

No. 17 He Means The World To Me

Aurora

He means the world to me.
At the start
With no prompting or persuasion, no particular occasion,
We'd, for no apparent reason, simply stop to tell each other,
You mean the world to me.

But as the years went by
We began
Once we'd set aside our play things, for all those adult day-to-day things,
Then, for some apparent reason, to no longer tell each other,
You mean the world to me.

You let those golden opportunities go by
You miss each precious chance to tell him you love him

How cruel the world can be.
Inch by inch
These new distances keep growing — day by day without our knowing

Till, for some apparent reason, he's inhabiting no longer
The same world as me.

Yet still, he still,
And I suppose he always will,
Mean everything to me ...

A silence between them. Carabosse is very affected by this. She brushes away a tear and tries vainly to pull herself together. Aurora, still deep in her thoughts, goes to take a bite of the apple.

Carabosse (*sharply*) Don't eat that!
Aurora (*startled*) What?
Narrators (*the front doorbell, again*) Brrriiinnnggg!
Aurora Oh, no! (*She puts the apple down on the coffee table. Rising*) Who on earth is it, now? Please, excuse me a moment.
Carabosse Of course.

Aurora goes off to the front door

Carabosse waits, listening. From off stage we hear Aurora and the Prince

Prince (*off*) Hallo, darling.
Aurora (*off*) Darling, what are you doing back at this time?
Prince (*off*) I was late again, you see. And they've given me the sack.
Aurora (*off*) They've what?
Prince (*off*) They've given me the sack, I'm afraid. The boot.
Aurora (*off, with a despairing wail*) Now what are we going to do ... (*She bursts into tears*)
Prince (*off, consoling her*) Oh, come on, old love ... there! there!
Aurora (*off*) We'll have no money ... no home ... nothing!
Carabosse Oh, for God's sake. I can't stand any more of this ...

The voices in the hall continue quietly under the next, as the Prince tries to calm Aurora. Carabosse, meanwhile, takes sudden decisive action. She takes up the apple and replaces it inside her briefcase. She takes out a heavy velvet drawstring bag and puts it on the table. Also a notebook on which she scrawls something and, tearing it off, she puts on top of the bag. She rises, looking for a way out, other than the front door

(*Glaring briefly at the sleeping triplets*) I'm going to regret this, you know! (*She looks out of the window*) Ah! Thank God for fire escapes!

Carabosse climbs out of the window taking her briefcase. She disappears. At the same moment, the Prince comes back with his arm round red-eyed Aurora, still sniffling

Prince ... no as I say, darling, I can probably get another job. Somewhere. I'll just have to do something else.
Aurora (*miserably*) But you can't do anything, that's the point ...
Prince Well, possibly not. That I do concede. (*Optimistically*) But what better time to learn, eh?
Aurora (*looking round*) Oh. Where is she? She's gone. (*Moving anxiously to the crib*) The boys are they ...? (*Seeing they are safe*) Oh, good.
Prince (*inspecting the note on the coffee table*) What on earth's this?
Aurora What?
Prince A note.
Aurora She must have left it. That woman.
Prince What woman?
Aurora What does it say?
Prince (*reading*) "The lucky winner". Very odd. Then there's this bag. Presumably she left this, too, whoever she was. What on earth is it? Heavy.

He opens the velvet bag. A bar of gold slides out on to the table. They stare at it

Aurora Oh. It's ...?
Prince Solid gold.
Aurora (*quite weak, suddenly*) Oh. Oh, oh, oh, oh, oh!

They both sit and stare at it, he on the sofa, she on the chair. Underscore starts: "This Has To Be Love"

It won't — suddenly start to melt or something, will it?
Prince Looks solid enough to me. Unless the roof starts leaking on it. (*He laughs*)
Aurora (*suddenly filled with love for him*) Oh, beloved!

She goes to sit by him hugging him

Prince What's that?

Aurora You mean the world to me. Do I mean the world to you?
Prince Oh, yes, rather. You are my world, you know that.
Aurora (*moved, clinging to him*) Oh.
Prince (*responding*) Wouldn't want to be anywhere else but here.

The underscore reaches a climax

Narrators And they all lived happily ever after!

This promises for a moment to be the end of the show. But then the lights fade and the scene changes

Epilogue

The interior of the cave

The rock has gone. All that's there is a saw bench with a scattering of sawdust round it and one or two off-cuts of wood. There is a mirror on the wall

Third Narrator But not quite everyone! Back at the cave, the Pigcutter who had given up all hope of Cara ever returning home again, with or without her wretched prince, had lost heart and abandoned work on his home improvements.
Fourth Narrator He had, of late, been given to retiring for long periods to his newly re-furnished bedroom where he lay for hours at a time on his recently completed bed, gazing up at his freshly decorated ceiling in a state of deep, deep depression.
Fifth Narrator Which explained the reason why, several afternoons later, he didn't at first hear his mistress returning.

Carabosse, tired and dusty, limps on, carrying her shoes, one with a broken heel. Her once smart business suit has also, like her, suffered the wear and tear of her journey. She stops and looks round the walls of the cave

Underscore creeps in under the next

Carabosse (*softly, in despair at what she sees*) Oh, no ...
Sixth Narrator And all of sudden, at that moment, it all caught up with her ...

First Narrator ... losing her beloved a part of her at least still desperately desired ...

Second Narrator ... and worse, feeling a certain pity for her beloved's pathetic little wife ...

Third Narrator ... and even worse than that, seeing those hideous triplets snuggled asleep in their crib, experiencing a moment of appalling maternal broodiness.

Fourth Narrator Having given away the last of her gold, she was now penniless ...

Fifth Narrator ... as a result she'd been ignominiously thrown out of her nasty cheap hotel with only the clothes she stood up in ...

Sixth Narrator ... and, with not a magic broomstick to her name, she had been forced to walk all the way home in her two hundred and ten pound, each, hand-made Italian shoes which were now totally and utterly ruined ...

First Narrator And, now she was home, to find the Pig apparently gone and seeing the DIY havoc he had wreaked in her absence. On every wall, row upon row of sagging, sloping shelves. Whichever way she turned, countless crooked un-closeable cupboards.

Second Narrator Experiencing this, Cara felt unfamiliar feelings welling up ...

Third Narrator ... feelings she had never before experienced ...

Fourth Narrator ... not in all the three hundred and something years of her life ...

Fifth Narrator ... never, never before!

Sixth Narrator And she stood in her once beautiful cave and cried out in despair.

Carabosse (*with a cry of pain*) PIG!!!! What have you done to my home?

Narrators And the witch burst into tears!

Carabosse starts to weep and wail loudly

The Pigcutter rushes on, alarmed by the disturbance. He sees Carabosse and, confused by her unfamiliar state, he runs to her concerned, but is afraid to touch her

Carabosse fades down under the next and continues wailing silently under

First Narrator Cara cried centuries of stored-up tears.

Second Narrator Tears she had never before been able, or indeed when she was a child had ever been allowed, to shed ...

In the ensuing dumb show, The Pigcutter dithers and runs out again. He returns, shortly, with a chair for her. It is one he has made and can hardly be described a thing of beauty. During the following, he is transformed back as the curse wears off. At this point he has lost his trotters and both his hands are restored, though he doesn't appear to notice

Third Narrator And as the Pigcutter flapped and flustered round her, wondering how best to cope with this unaccustomed situation ...

Whilst she cries on, blindly oblivious, he seats her gently in the chair. He dithers some more

Then he runs off again, briefly

Fourth Narrator And once the witch had exhausted a lifetime of tears, her crying still continued ...
Fifth Narrator But it wasn't tears now she wept, but instead freezing cold liquid ...
Sixth Narrator It was water melting from the ice previously frozen around her heart.

The Pigcutter returns with a crudely-shaped coffee table, gently placing Carabosse's feet on it. He has now regained his human features, too

First Narrator And, as suddenly as it had started, her crying ceased. She had nothing left inside her to cry.

Carabosse takes one or two deep breaths

Carabosse (*more herself again*) Whoo. That's better out than in.
Pigcutter (*concerned*) All right?
Carabosse Yes. I think so. What this I'm sitting on?
Pigcutter It's a chair.
Carabosse A chair? Since when did we own a chair?
Pigcutter I made it for you. Do you like it?
Carabosse No, it's bloody uncomfortable.

She is aware of her improvised footstool

(*Removing her feet from it*) What the hell's this?
Pigcutter It's a table. I made that as well.

Carabosse A table? I can't eat off that, can I?
Pigcutter No, it's a coffee table.
Carabosse (*angrily*) A coffee table? *A coffee table*? What do we want with a sodding coffee table, you arsehole? Take it away, go on!

The Pigcutter grabs up the table hastily

Take it away at once, you stupid brainless, snout faced — (*Noticing the change in him for the first time*) What's happened to your face?

The Pigcutter puts down the coffee table

Pigcutter (*feeling his face*) My face? How do you mean?
Carabosse Where are your trotters?
Pigcutter My hands! I got my hands back. My face? Has my face come back? (*He moves away to look at himself in the mirror. Looking at himself*) It has!
Carabosse Did you put up that revolting mirror?
Pigcutter It's come back! I got my face back!
Carabosse That's got to go, as well! You know how I feel about mirrors.
Pigcutter How do I look, then? What do you think?
Carabosse What?
Pigcutter My new face? Do you like it?
Carabosse You don't look all that different to me.
Pigcutter Don't I? (*Turning back to the mirror, sadly*) No, I don't suppose I do really. Over the years, I used to imagine I did.
Carabosse (*barely listening to him*) I must have got my powers back, as well ...
Pigcutter You know, while I was looking like a pig, I sort of grew to imagine that once I got changed back, I'd look a bit like a handsome prince. You know, as if I'd been a frog.

Carabosse stabs her hand at the mirror, testing her powers

Narrators Waaaaahhhhh! (*As a breaking mirror*) Smash! Tinkle! Tinkle!

The Pigcutter jumps back, dodging the glass

Carabosse Yes, that's working!
Pigcutter Seven years' bad luck, that.
Carabosse (*gloomily*) Who's counting?

Pigcutter No, I never looked like a prince. Ever. I just — looked like me. Probably why my wife walked out. (*He sighs*) Oh, well. Cheerio, then.

Carabosse Where are you going?

Pigcutter I've no idea.

Carabosse You're not walking out.

Pigcutter Well, I thought with the curse being lifted ...

Carabosse You're staying here.

Pigcutter Why?

Carabosse Because, I say so!

Pigcutter Why, what's there to stay for? You can't make me stay.

Carabosse (*dangerously, raising her hand*) Try me.

Pigcutter That's not going to work! You tried that with him. Lover boy. Look where that got you. You couldn't make him stay, could you? Not with all your powers.

She doesn't move

(*Bravely*) Go on then do your worst. See if I care. What can you do to me, eh? Have me walking round here for the rest of my life with a bag on my head? Turn me into a beetle? Then who're you going to have to talk to, eh?

Carabosse drops her hand slowly

Listen, you don't want me here. You're glamorous. Go and find yourself another prince. You can pull one, easy, looking like that. You're knockout. You'll have no problem with princes. They'll be queuing round your — cave.

Silence

You don't want me now, do you? I mean, come on, look at me. Look.

Slight pause

(*Laughing*) Tell you what, I've got an idea. Couple of years, if I'm smart, make a bit of money selling my furniture, I could perhaps save up, go to that place of yours, have a make-over myself. You know, get a spot of magic done on myself, transform into a handsome prince.

Carabosse (*softly*) Don't you fucking dare!

Pause. Underscore starts

Pigcutter If you really want me to stay, you could always try a bit of good old fashioned magic, see if that works.

Carabosse (*slightly suspiciously*) What's that?

Pigcutter You could ask me, nicely.

Carabosse *Nicely?*

Pigcutter Yes. Nicely. Come on. You can do nicely, if you try. Come on, have a go. Nicely, now.

Carabosse opens and closes her mouth, for once lost for words

Come on, girl, you can do it!

Carabosse (*floundering*) I … I'm … I … I'll ... (*She sings*)

No. 18 I'll Settle For You

I'll settle for you.
Till Mr Right walks through my door,
Six foot six, with big square jaw
His knuckles dragging on the floor,

Pigcutter I'll settle for you
Until a dizzy blonde appears,
Nothing much between her ears,
And pleads with me in floods of tears,

Carabosse Till pigs start flying,
Till birds lose their song,

Pigcutter Till fish start crying,

Both You'll do till something better comes along.

Carabosse You'll just have to do
Till you become a total pain
Till your jokes drive me insane
Till I fall out of love again
But till I do

Both I'll settle for you.

Pigcutter I'll give you my all,
My tender, loving, beating heart,
Not a lot, still it's a start,

Carabosse Yeah, what about your other part?
I'll give you the lot
I'm yours for better or for worse

Pigcutter Filthy tempered and perverse,
You lie and cheat and swear and curse
But I adore you, your sweet warts and all.
Carabosse I'll be here for you
At least till your attraction starts to pall.

Both I'll settle for you.
Through rain and sunshine, come what may,
We both wither and decay,
Now and forever and a day,
Just we two
I'll settle for you.
And I hope you'll agree
If I'm happy to settle for you,
Then you — you'll settle with me!

They both finish rather jubilantly. Carabosse gives one of her old-style laughs

Carabosse Ha- ha-ha-ha-ha-ha!
Pigcutter That's my girl!

They embrace

Black-out

END OF PLAY

FURNITURE AND PROPERTY LIST

Dressing may be added at the director's discretion

PROLOGUE

On stage: Nil

Off stage: Bed. *On it*: bedclothes (**Stage Management**)

Personal: **Prince**: crown, sword
Aurora: crown, necklace, rings

ACT I
SCENE 1

On stage: Rock

Off stage: Besom broom (**Pigcutter**)
2 very dirty tin mugs of dark liquid (**Pigcutter**)
Besom broom (**Pigcutter**)

Personal: **Prince**: pair of rose-tinted spectacles, crown, bag over head, sword

SCENE 2

On stage: Nil

Off stage: Broomstick (**Carabosse**)
2 seats, one with vicious-looking metal spikes (**Stage Management**)

SCENE 3

On stage: Nil

Personal: **Aurora**: crown, necklace, rings

SCENE 4

On stage: Rock

Off stage: Sack of gold (**Pigcutter**)

SCENE 5

On stage: Nil

Off stage: Bag of gold (**Carabosse**)

Personal: **Prince**: crown, sword
Aurora: crown, necklace, rings
Woman 1: mobile phone
Man 1: mobile phone
Woman 2: mobile phone
Man 2: mobile phone
Woman 3: mobile phone
Man 3: mobile phone
Woman 4: mobile phone
Man 4: mobile phone
Woman 5: mobile phone
Man 5: mobile phone
Woman 6: mobile phone

SCENE 6

On stage: 2 chairs in reception area

Off stage: Bag of gold (**Carabosse**)

Personal: **Prince**: purse, paper crown, paper sword
Aurora: paper crown, paper necklace, paper rings

SCENE 7

On stage: Chairs in reception area

Off stage: Couch (**Stage Management**)

Personal: **Carabosse**: bag containing gold bars
Assistant: watch

ACT II
Scene 1

On stage: Nil

Off stage: Case of marmalade (**Prince**)
Trayload of iced lagers (**Aurora**)
Couch (**Stage Management**)
Full-length mirror (**Beauticians**)
Clipboard (**Miss Chasum**)

Scene 2

On stage: Nil

Off stage: Hospital bed with bedclothes (**Stage Management**)

Scene 3

On stage: Nil

Off stage: Bag of gold (**Carabosse**)
Brown paper bag (**Pigcutter**)

Scene 4

On stage: Narrow bed. *On it*: bedclothes
Triple crib containing 3 small babies

Scene 5

On stage: Checkout till
Chair
Magazine for **Girl**
Shelves
Pyramid of cans of peas

Off stage: Bag of gold (**Carabosse**)
Large cardboard carton filled with cans of peas (**Prince**)

SCENE 6

On stage: Battered sofa
Armchair
Radio or music unit

Off stage: Bag of gold (**Carabosse**)
Large cardboard carton filled with cans of peas (**Prince**)
Glass of water (**Carabosse**)

SCENE 7

On stage: Sofa
Armchair
Small low table
Crib with 3 small babies

Off stage: Briefcase containing red apple, heavy velvet drawstring bag with gold bar inside, notebook and pen (**Carabosse**)

EPILOGUE

On stage: Saw bench. *Around it*: sawdust
Off-cuts of wood
Mirror on wall

Off stage: Pair of shoes, one with broken heel (**Carabosse**)
Ill-made chair (**Pigcutter**)
Crudely-shaped coffee table (**Pigcutter**)

LIGHTING PLOT

Property fittings required: nil

PROLOGUE

To open: Bring up general lighting

Cue 1 At the conclusion of the overture (Page 1)
Fade to black-out

Cue 2 Dramatic opening chord (Page 1)
Bring up lighting on **Narrators** *(each lit individually as they speak)*

Cue 3 **First Narrator**: "… watched and gloated." (Page 1)
Spot on **Carabosse**

Cue 4 **Carabosse**: "Ha-ha-ha-ha-ha-ha!" (Page 1)
Cut spot on **Carabosse**

Cue 5 **First Narrator**: "And she laughed and laughed ..." (Page 2)
Spot on **Carabosse**

Cue 6 **Carabosse**: "Ha-ha-ha-ha-ha-ha!" (Page 2)
Cut spot on **Carabosse**

Cue 7 The **Prince** enters (Page 2)
Bring up lighting on **Prince**

Cue 8 **First Narrator**: "... witch watched wickedly ..." (Page 3)
Spot on **Carabosse**

Cue 9 **Carabosse**: "Ha-ha-ha-ha-ha-ha!" (Page 3)
Cut spot on **Carabosse**

Cue 10 **First Narrator**: "Even the wicked witch was impressed..." (Page 3)
Spot on **Carabosse**

Cue 11 **Carabosse**: "Ooooh!" (Page 3)
Cut spot on **Carabosse**

Cue 12 **Prince**: "Ha! Ha!" (Page 3)
Reduce lighting to concentrate on **Prince**

Cue 13	As the **Prince** reaches the individual **Narrators** *Bring up lighting on individual* **Narrators** *in sequence*	(Page 4)
Cue 14	Bed rises up with **Princess Aurora** on it *Bring up lighting on bed*	(Page 5)
Cue 15	**Prince**: (singing) "This certainly has to be love!" *Spot on* **Carabosse**	(Page 5)
Cue 16	**Carabosse**: "Yuurrrkkk!" *Cut spot on* **Carabosse**	(Page 5)
Cue 17	**Prince**: (singing) "It's got to be, has to be love!" *Spot on* **Carabosse**	(Page 5)
Cue 18	**Carabosse**: "Yuurrrkkk!" (Second time) *Cut spot on* **Carabosse**	(Page 5)
Cue 19	**Aurora**: (singing) "This certainly has to be love!" *Spot on* **Carabosse**	(Page 6)
Cue 20	**Carabosse**: "Ha-ha-ha-ha-ha-ha!" *Cut spot on* **Carabosse**	(Page 8)

ACT I, SCENE 1

To open: Dim lighting on cave area

Cue 21	The **Pigcutter** goes out after **Carabosse** and the **Prince** *Crossfade to spot on* **Aurora**	(Page 22)
Cue 22	**Aurora** bursts into tears and goes off *Crossfade to dim lighting on cave area*	(Page 22)
Cue 23	**Fifth Narrator**: " And while the Prince ..." *Fade to black-out*	(Page 26)

ACT I, SCENE 2

To open: Dim, shadowy lighting on cavern area

Cue 24	A crestfallen **Carabosse** is alone *Bring up lighting on* **Pigcutter**	(Page 31)

ACT I, SCENE 3

To open: Sunlight

No cues

ACT I, SCENE 4

To open: Dim lighting on cave area

No cues

ACT, SCENE 5

To open: General overcast exterior lighting

No cues

ACT I, SCENE 6

To open: General lighting on reception area

Cue 25	The **Prince** and **Aurora** go out *Crossfade to mouth of cave*	(Page 44)
Cue 26	The **Pigcutter** goes in *Fade to black-out*	(Page 44)

ACT I, SCENE 7

To open: Bright interior lighting

Cue 27	**Carabosse** gives a cackling laugh *Black-out*	(Page 48)

ACT II, SCENE 1

To open: General lighting

No cues

ACT II, Scene 2

To open: General interior lighting

No cues

ACT II, Scene 3

To open: General exterior lighting

No cues

ACT II, Scene 4

To open: Dim lighting from street lamp light source through window

Cue 28 The **Prince** switches on the light (Page 68)
Bring up interior lighting

ACT II, Scene 5

To open: General lighting

Cue 29 The cash till and display go (Page 73)
Cross fade to lighting on mouth of the cave

Cue 30 The **Pigcutter** goes back in again, rather sadly (Page 73)
Fade to black-out

ACT II, Scene 6

To open: Dim interior lighting

Cue 31 **Carabosse** switches on the light (Page 73)
Bring up interior lighting

Cue 32 **Carabosse** fiddles with the light (Page 75)
Increase, then decrease lighting to lower than opening

Cue 33 **Carabosse** goes out (Page 76)
Fade to black-out

ACT II, Scene 7

To open: General interior lighting

Cue 34 **Narrators**: "And they all lived happily ever after!" (Page 82)
Fade to black-out

EPILOGUE

To open: Dim lighting

Cue 35 **Pigcutter**: "That's my girl!" They embrace (Page 88)
Black-out

EFFECTS PLOT

The sound effects in the play are provided by the **Narrators**.